On the drag

The football grounds of...

SUFFOLK

by Steven Penny
in association with

First published in Great Britain in December 2024
Reprinted January 2025

Copyright – Steven Penny 2024
Penny for your Sports Publications

ISBN: 978-1-7392267-3-2

Unless stated, pictures are by the author.
Cover photographs:
Front – Clockwise from top left: Beccles Caxton, Ipswich Town,
Brantham Athletic and Lakenheath
Back – main image: Whitton United. Insets, from top left: Stanton,
Lowestoft Town, Cornard United, Hadleigh United,
Mildenhall Town and Spexhall Huntsman & Hounds

steve@stevepennymedia.co.uk – https://tinyurl.com/spennymedia

A **Penny** for your **Sports** production

Contents

Gone but not forgotten **142**

Other grounds **144**

League placings 2008-2024 . . . . **162**

That's champion! **163**

Other leagues **166**

The Offside Trust

The Offside Trust is committed to supporting survivors of abuse, not only in football but in all sports and daily life.

The trust's motto is that kids can grow up as kids in a safe and supportive environment.

The Offside Trust was formed in 2017 by Steve Walters, Chris Unsworth and other survivors of abuse, and is run by three directors, assisted by volunteers.

More than 7,000 have been helped by trust to get assistance for their abuse via many organisations that are signposted for people to contact, including MIND, Childline and Samaritans.

Free awareness days, abuse and awareness seminars are run and the trust provides such things as captain's armbands and logos for banners to put up at clubs at all levels of the game.

The trust is fully committed to supporting anyone who contact them. Abuse still exists and is prevalent in all areas.

If your club, academy or league would like to get involved and host a free abuse and awareness seminar, please email *alan.offsidetrust@gmail.com* for more information.

See also pages 184/185.

Football in Suffolk

Ipswich Town's incredible rise to the Premier League has heralded an increase in interest in football across Suffolk but Portman Road can only house a limited number of fans.

Away tickets are hard to get hold of and many fixtures are not played on the traditional Saturday afternoon, so fans keen to maintain their regular footie fix are looking to the lower levels to meet that need. This book will help.

It takes you on a trip around 50-plus senior grounds, whether you are a Tractorboy in search of live action on a blank Saturday date, a casual fan or a groundhopper. Many grounds are within easy walking distance of railway stations for those not travelling by car. The nearest railway station listed is not necessarily the closest to the ground but the nearest one with public transport available if not within walking distance.

This is not a comprehensive record of the history of football in Suffolk but gives you a taste of the county's football pedigree.

Clubs are set out in descending league order, with brief details about the grounds, plus badge and shirt colours. For the exact centre spot of the ground you are seeking, use the What3Words app – this is free to download.

Although the book is devoted to Suffolk clubs and grounds and clubs, Bungay Town (whose ground is across the border in Norfolk), Kings Park Rangers (an Essex club playing in Suffolk) and Thetford Rovers (a Norfolk club playing in Suffolk) are included.

Suffolk clubs play in a wide variety of leagues, stretching across the country. Ipswich are, of course, in national competition, but further down the pyramid, Needham Market, in National League North, travel as far afield as Oxford City and South Shields. Many clubs are in the Eastern Counties League and face trips across to Lincolnshire and Essex while, even at local levels, teams in the Suffolk & Ipswich League and Anglian Combination face some lengthy cross-county journeys.

Traditional names of leagues and stadiums are used throughout the book. I do recognise the valuable part sponsors play in the game but, for ease of reference and to avoid confusion, sponsored names are not used.

Many lower level 'senior' grounds are little more than fenced off pitches so some of the capacities listed are vague. Several are 'portable' grounds – literally a field with the necessary furniture – goalposts, dug outs, fence surround, etc – added purely for matchday. There is nothing to see at other times so beware 'popping in' on the off-chance of some pictures while you are in the area.

The book focuses on the 51 'senior' teams – that is those that qualify to play in the Suffolk FA Premier or Senior Cups. The lowest senior level in the county is Division One of the Anglian Combination – the only one of the county's feeder leagues to have two senior tiers. Despite their name, Senior Divisions A and B of the Cambs League are classed as junior football – as are the second tiers of the other feeder leagues.

Spread across other divisions and leagues are dozens more teams. They mainly play on park pitches but there are some hidden gems to discover – make sure you get to see a game at Beccles Caxton or Stanton, for a real surprise of a ground for the level they currently play.

Why 'On the drag'? The last year or so has involved many Saturday afternoon dashes, trying to catch the lower-level clubs while they were 'fully dressed'. That regularly meant getting to more than one match – pre-match at one, first-half at another, second-half at the next and, if I was lucky, the end of another. I was caught out at Grundisburgh after arriving just before kick-off and managing to park in the corner of the car park. Unfortunately, when I came to leave after 20 minutes, my car had been blocked in. I eventually found the driver, who was reluctant to move it but eventually did so. It meant I was running late for the remaining two matches. In both cases, I was greeted at the gate by club officials telling me I was "on the drag". It's a similar Suffolk expression to "on the huh" – as some of my wonky pictures might confirm!

All information is believed to be correct for the start of the 2024/25 season.

Steven Penny,
Lowestoft, December 2024

Abbreviations:	
1C – Division One Central	Ln – Lane
1Q, 2Q, 3Q, 4Q –1st, 2nd, 3rd, 4th qualifying round	Mdw – Meadow
	Mkt – Market
Acad – Academy	ND – North Division
AFA – Amateur Football Association	OSM – Old St Mary's
	Pav – Pavilion
AFC - Amalgamated Football Club	Prem – Premier
Ath – Athletic	Prem Cen –Prem Division Central
Ave – Avenue	PF – Playing Fields
c – circa (about)	RCYS – Roman Catholic Youth Club
Cen – Centre	
Co's – Counties	Rd – Road
CWS – Cooperative Wholesale Society	Rec – Recreation Ground
	Res – Reserves
Dev – Development	Rgrs – Rangers
Dist – District	Rov – Rovers
Div – Division	S&SC – Sports & Social Club
ECL – Eastern Counties League	SC – Sports Centre
FA – Football Association	SG – Sports Ground
Gt – Great	SL – Southern League
IL – Isthmian League	Svcs – Services
IOGT – International Order of Good Templars	Tn – Town
	Utd – United
	W Div – West Division

The pyramid

A pathway to the very top of English football has been put in place over recent decades. It means that, subject to meeting various ground criteria for each step up, it is theoretically possible for any club to work their way from newly formed to the Premier League.

The 'Level 1' giants of the multi-million pound superstar world are at the top of the pyramid and below them stretches more than 20 tiers to true parks football.

Subject to regular ground improvements at their Normanston Park venue (and a bottomless money pot), Lowestoft League Division Three side Flying Dutchman could be playing in the Anglian Combination within three seasons and, thanks to that league being condensed into regional sections, be taking on Framlingham Town four seasons later in the Eastern Counties League.

Carry on building and spending, and National League North derby dates with Needham Market can be booked for the 2035/36 season. From there, and with the backing of a rich sheikh or two no doubt, it is a mere five leaps to a regular date at Old Trafford and matches against the likes of Liverpool and Arsenal. Yes, Flying Dutchman could be in the Premier League as soon as 2040! They can but dream...

Level	Suffolk clubs
1: FA Premier League	1
2: Championship	0
3: League One	0
4: League Two	0
5: National League	0
6: National League North	1
7: Isthmian League and Southern League Premier	3
8: Isthmian League and Southern League Division One	5
9: Eastern Counties League Premier Division	8
10: Eastern Counties League Division One	8
11: Feeder leagues – Anglian Combination, Suffolk/Ipswich League, Cambs League, Essex & Suffolk Border League top division	21
12: Feeder leagues second tier	23
13: Feeder leagues third tier	17
14: Feeder leagues fourth tier	19
15: Feeder leagues fifth tier	19
16: Feeder leagues sixth tier	18
17: Support leagues – Lowestoft League, Central & S Norfolk League, etc) top division	6
18: Support leagues second tier	7
19: Support leagues third tier	5
Outside pyramid (Veterans and Services leagues)	50-plus

Suffolk's senior football clubs

 1 Ipswich Town

 2 Needham Market

 3 AFC Sudbury
4 Leiston
5 Lowestoft Town

 6 Bury Town
7 Felixstowe & Walton United
8 Ipswich Wanderers
9 Mildenhall Town
10 Newmarket Town

 11 Brantham Athletic
12 Hadleigh United
13 Kirkley & Pakefield
14 Lakenheath
15 Long Melford
16 Stowmarket Town
17 Walsham-le-Willows
18 Woodbridge Town

 3 AFC Sudbury Reserves
19 Cornard United
20 Framlingham Town
21 Haverhill Borough
22 Haverhill Rovers
4 Leiston Under 23s
2 Needham Market Reserves
23 Whitton United

 24 Bacton United '89
25 Beccles Town
26 Bungay Town
27 Coplestonians
28 Debenham Leisure Centre
29 East Bergholt United
30 Grundisburgh
31 Halesworth Town
32 Haughley United
33 Henley Athletic
19 Kings Park Rangers
34 Leiston St Margaret's
10 Newmarket Town Reserves
35 Old Newton United
36 Sporting '87
37 Stowupland Falcons
3 Sudbury Sports
38 Tattingstone United
39 Trimley St Mary
40 Waveney
41 Wickham Market

 42 Brandon Town
13 Kirkley & Pakefield Reserves
43 Mutford & Wrentham
44 Thetford Rovers

 Railway station

 Major road

Suffolk's senior football clubs

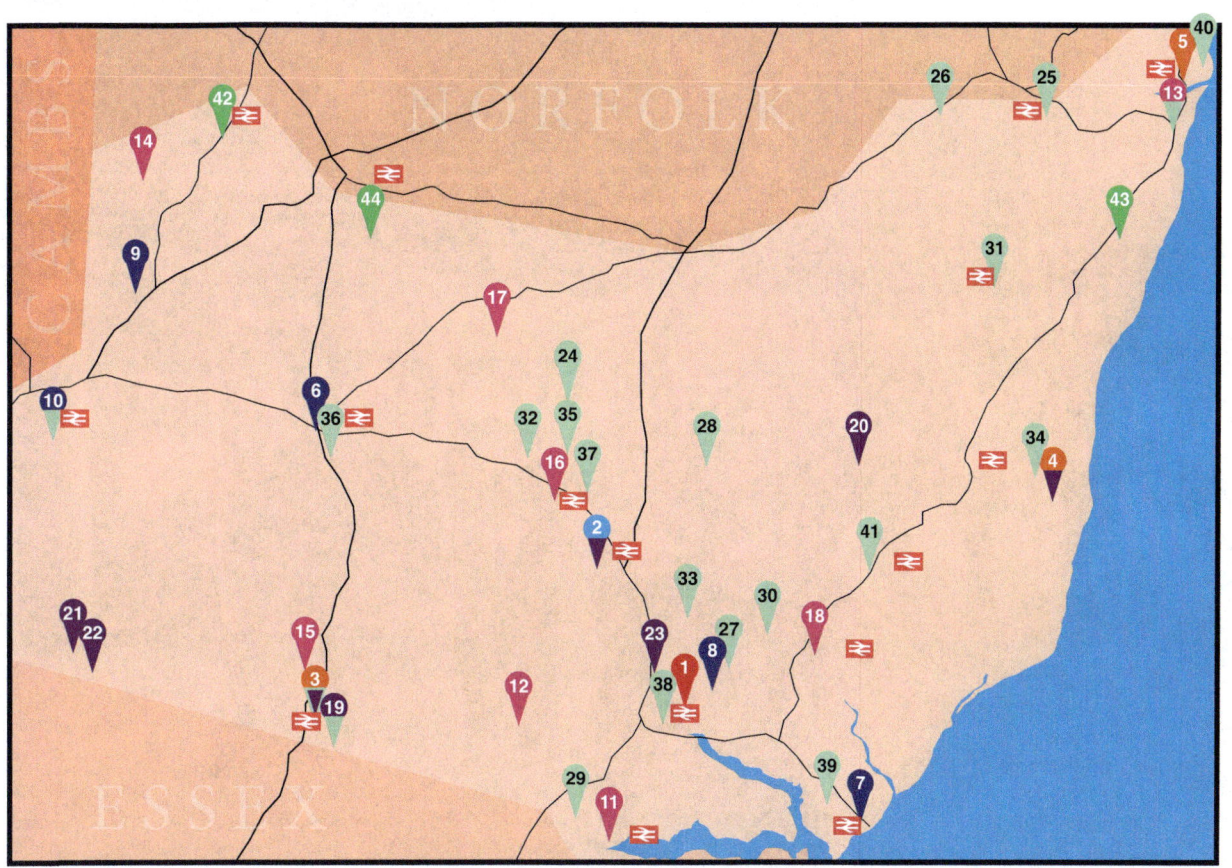

Ipswich Town returned to the Premier League in 2024 after a 23-year absence.

Picture: June Essex/Football Weekends

Ipswich Town

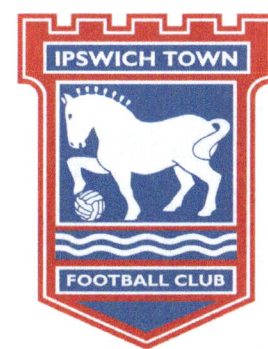

Current league:
Premier League

Formed: 1878 (as Ipswich AFC. Town suffix added in 1888)

Ground address: Portman Road, Ipswich, IP1 2DA

 Centre spot reference:
window.exchanges.state

Nearest railway station:
Ipswich – 10-minute walk

Capacity: 30,014

Record crowd: 38,010 v Leeds United, FA Cup 1974/5

Admission price: £38 (£34)

Car parking: Town centre car parks

Club shop: Yes

Refreshments: Yes **Bar:** Yes

Programme: £3.50

 *itfc.co.uk*

 */officialitfc*

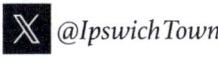 *@IpswichTown*

League history: Norfolk/Suffolk 1899-1903, 1906-7; SE Anglian 1903-06; Southern Amateur 1907-35; Eastern Counties 1935-36; Southern 1936-37; Football League 1938-92, 1995-2000, 2002-2024; Premier League 1992-95, 2000-02, 2024-date
Major honours: Football League champions 1961/2
Division Two champions 1960/1, 67/8, 91/2
Division Three South champions 1953/4, 56/7
Southern League champions 1936/7
Southern Amateur champs 1921/2, 29/30, 32/3, 33/4
Best cup runs – FA Cup: Winners 1977/8
League Cup: Semi-final 1981/2, 84/5, 2000/1, 10/1
European Cup: Second round 1962/3
UEFA Cup: Winners 1980/1
European Cup Winners Cup: Quarter-final 1978/9
Anglo-Italian Cup Quarter-final 1995/6
FA Amateur Cup Semi-final 1901/2

Portman Road is again hosting top-flight matches, rekindling the 1970s glory years under Bobby Robson.

Ipswich Town

Picture: June Essex

Aiming high: An aerial view across Needham Market's two grounds – the academy arena, foreground, and main stadium.
Picture: Ben Pooley Photography

Current league:
National League North

Formed: 1919

Ground address: Bloomfields, Quinton Road,
Needham Market, Ipswich, IP6 8DA

 Centre spot reference:
guidebook.sample.decrease

Nearest railway station:
Needham Market – 10-minute walk

Capacity: 3,000

Record crowd: 1,748 v Cambridge United,
FA Cup 2013/14

Admission price: £15

Car parking: Large car park at ground

Club shop: Yes

Refreshments: Yes

Bar: Yes

Programme: £3

 needhammarketfc.co.uk

 */needhammktfc*

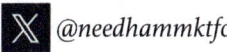 *@needhammktfc*

Needham Market

League history: Suffolk & Ipswich League 1921-95;
Eastern Counties League 1996-2010;
Isthmian League 2010-18; Southern League 2018-24;
National League 2024-date

Major honours: Southern League Premier Division
Central champions 2023/24
Isthmian League Division One North champions
2014/5
Eastern Counties League champions 2009/10
Suffolk & Ipswich League champions 1995/6

Best cup runs – FA Cup: First round 2022/3
FA Trophy: Quarter-final: 2021/2
FA Vase: Semi-final: 2007/8

Needham Market

Needham's Bloomfields ground has developed alongside the club's rise from the Suffolk & Ipswich League

Current league:
Southern League, Premier Division Central

Formed: 1999 (an amalgamation of Sudbury Town, 1885, and Sudbury Wanderers, 1958)

Ground address: Brundon Lane, Sudbury, CO10 7HN

 Centre spot reference:
universes.weddings.maddening

Nearest railway station:
Sudbury – 30-minute walk

Capacity: 2,500

Record crowd: 2,000 v Colchester United, FA Cup 2021/22

Admission price: £12 (£7 women's games)

Car parking: At ground

Club shop: Limited stock

Refreshments: Yes

Bar: Yes

Programme: Online only

 afcsudbury.co.uk

 */AFCSudburyOfficial*

 *@AFCSudbury*

AFC Sudbury

League history: Eastern Counties 1999-2006; Isthmian 2006-08, 2010-23; Southern 2008-10, 2023-date (Sudbury Town – W Suffolk League; SE Anglian League; Colchester League; Bury League 1919-21, 23-28, 33-38; E Anglian League; Essex Suffolk Border League 1912-14, 22-31, 36-55; Haverhill League 1919-22, 28-33; Suffolk & Ipswich League 1921-23, 31-36; Eastern Counties League 1955-1990, 1997-99; Southern League 1990-97) (Sudbury Wanderers – Halstead League 1958-59; Essex & Suffolk Border League 1959-91; ECL 1991-99)

Major honours: Isthmian League Division One North champions 2015/6. Eastern Counties League champions 2000/1, 01/2, 02/3, 03/4, 04/5 (and 1973/4, 74/5, 75/6, 85/6, 86/7, 88/9 and 89/90 as Sudbury Town). Suffolk & Ipswich League champions as Sudbury Town 1934/5, 52/3. Essex & Suffolk Border League champions as Sudbury Town 1948/9, 49/50, 51/2, 52/3, 53/4. As Sudbury Town Reserves 1980/1. As Sudbury Wanderers 1989/90, 90/1. As AFC Sudbury Reserves 1999/2000, 2001/2

Best cup runs – FA Cup: First round 2000/1, 21/2 (Second round as Sudbury Town 1996/7)
FA Trophy: Second round 2016/7 (Third round as Sudbury Tn 1995/6)
FA Vase: Final 2002/3, 03/4, 04/5 (and 1988/9 as Sudbury Town)

Sudbury Town moved in with Sudbury Wanderers in 1999 to become Amalgamated Football Club (AFC) Sudbury.

AFC Sudbury

Leiston

Current league:
Southern League, Premier Division Central

Formed: 1880 as Leiston Town (known as Leiston Works Athletic 1919-35)

Ground address: Town Athletic Association, Victory Road, Leiston, IP16 4DQ

 Centre spot reference: inflict.innocence.envy

Nearest railway station:
Saxmundham – five miles away

Capacity: 2,250

Record crowd: 1,250 v Fleetwood, FA Cup 2008/09

Admission price: £12

Car parking: At ground and nearby streets

Club shop: Yes

Refreshments: Yes

Bar: Yes

Programme: £2.50

 leistonfc.co.uk

 /LeistonFootballClub

 @leistonfc

League history: N Suffolk League 1894-1909; Suffolk & Ipswich League 1900–04, 12-14; 19-21, 26-48, 53-2001; East Anglian League 1904-7, 11-20; Essex & Suffolk Border League 1920-21; Norfolk & Suffolk League 1921-26, 48-53; Eastern Counties League 2001-11; Isthmian League 2011-18; Southern League 2018-date

Major honours: Isthmian League Division One North champions 2011/2
Eastern Counties League champions 2010/1
Suffolk & Ipswich League champions 1900/01, 01/2, 02/3

Best cup runs – FA Cup: First round 2008/9
FA Trophy: Fourth round 2022/3
FA Vase: Quarter-final 2010/1

Leiston were one of only three Suffolk Full members of the FA from the 1950s until 1982, along with Ipswich Town and Lowestoft Town.

Lowestoft Town

Current league:
Southern League, Premier Division Central

Formed: 1887 (East Suffolk merged with Kirkley to form Lowestoft FC in 1887, they added the Town suffix in 1890. Town merged with another Kirkley in 1935)

Ground address: Crown Meadow, Love Road, Lowestoft, NR32 2PA

 Centre spot reference: most.places.joke

Nearest railway station:
Lowestoft – 10-minute walk

Capacity: 3,000

Record crowd: 5,000 v Watford, FA Cup 1967/8

Admission price: £13

Car parking: Town centre car parks and streets

Club shop: Yes **Refreshments:** Yes **Bar:** Yes

Programme: £2

 lowestofttownfc.co.uk

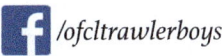 /ofcltrawlerboys

 @ofcltrawlerboys

League history: North Suffolk League 1894-97; Norfolk & Suffolk League 1897-1935; Eastern Counties League 1935-2009; Isthmian League 2009-2013, 2016-18, 2022-24; National League 2013-2016; Southern League 2018-22, 24-date

Major honours: Isthmian League Division One North champions 2009/10, 2023/4. Eastern Counties League champions 1935/6, 37/8, 62/3, 64/5, 65/6, 66/7, 67/8, 79/70, 70/1, 77/8, 2005/6, 08/9. Norfolk & Suffolk League champions 1897/8, 98/9, 1900/1, 01/2, 02/3, 03/4, 28/9, 30/1. Anglian Combination champions (Reserves) 1957/8, 77/8, 79/80

Best cup runs – FA Cup: First round 1926/7, 38/9, 66/7, 67/8, 77/8, 2009/10
FA Trophy: Second round 1971/2
FA Vase: Final 2007/8
FA Amateur Cup: Final 1899/1900

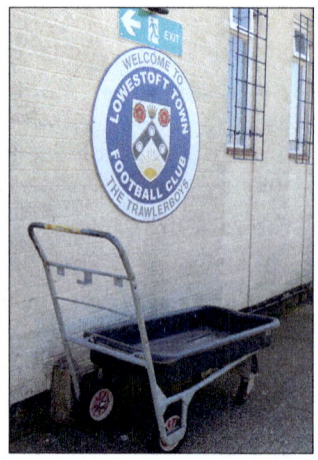

Going Dutch? Crown Meadow is the furthest east of all the UK's senior stadiums.

Lowestoft Town

NO STANDING IN THIS AREA

Thank you

THE TEA H

TEA / COFFEE
BOVRIL £1·50
HOT CHOCOLATE

SOUP £1·50

CHOCOLATE BARS

CRISPS £1

CANS £1·50

WATER £1

LUCOZADE
SPORT £2·00
CARLING / DOOM BAR £3

THANK YOU FOR
YOUR SUPPORT
THIS SEASON

Current league:
Isthmian League, North Division

Formed: 1872 (known as Bury St Edmunds 1872-85, 95-1908 and Bury United 1908-23)

Ground address: Ram Meadow, Cotton Lane, Bury St Edmunds, IP33 1XT

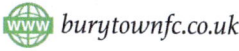 **Centre spot reference:** buzzards.troll.purple

Nearest railway station: Bury St Edmunds – 15-minute walk

Capacity: 3,500

Record crowd: 2,480 v Enfield, FA Cup 1986/87 (4,343 at previous ground – King's Road – v Cambridge Town, FA Cup, 1949/50)

Admission price: £11

Car parking: Large pay & display at ground

Club shop: Yes

Refreshments: Yes **Bar:** Yes **Programme:** £2

 *burytownfc.co.uk*

/BuryTownFootballClub

 *@BuryTownFC*

Bury Town

League history: Norfolk & Suffolk League 1899-1902, 20-29, 32-35; Sth East Anglia League 1904-1914; Essex & Suffolk Border League 1929-32; Eastern Counties League 1935-64, 76-87, 96-2006; Metropolitan League 1964-71; Southern League 1971-76, 87-96, 2008-10; Isthmian League 2006-08, 10-date

Major honours: Southern League Division One Midlands champions 2009/10
Metropolitan League champions 1965/6, 68/9
Eastern Counties League champions 1963/4

Best cup runs – FA Cup: First round: 1968/9, 2008/9
FA Trophy: Second round: 1970/1
FA Vase: Semi-final: 2005/6

Bury Town moved to Ram Meadow in 1978 from the Kings Road ground that had been home for more than a century.

Bury Town

Current league:
Isthmian League, North Division

Formed: 2000 (also known as Felixstowe 1890-1902, Felixstowe United 1945-52, Felixstowe Town changed to Felixstowe Port & Town in 1996 and merged with Walton United, formed 1895, in 2000)

Ground address: Dellwood Avenue, Felixstowe, IP11 9HT

 Centre spot reference: cone.dirt.pillow

Nearest railway station:
Felixstowe – 10-minute walk

Capacity: 2,160

Record crowd: 2,350, friendly v Ipswich Town 2023/24

Admission price: £10

Car parking: At ground and streets

Club shop: Yes

Refreshments: Yes **Bar:** Yes

Programme: Online only

 felixstowefootball.co.uk

 /OfficialSeasiders

 @Felixseasiders

Felixstowe & Walton Utd

League history: Suffolk & Ipswich League 1896-1901, 1902-12, 23-66; Essex & Suffolk Border League 1966-76; Eastern Counties League 1976-2018; Isthmian League 2018-date

Major honours: Suffolk & Ipswich League champions as Felixstowe Town 1910/1, 36/7, 57/8, 64/5 and as Walton United 1913/4, 20/1, 25/6.

Best cup runs – FA Cup: 3Q 2016/7
FA Trophy: Second round 2020/21, 21/2
FA Vase: Third round 1978/9, 80/1, 91/2

Felixstowe's original stand had to be remodelled and reversed when the club moved from what is now the car park to the pitch behind it.

Felixstowe & Walton United

Current league:
Isthmian League, North Division

Formed: 1980 (as Loadwell Ipswich, changed name 1989. Also known as Lancaster Ipswich)

Ground address: Humber Doucy Lane, Ipswich, IP4 3NR

 **Centre spot reference:** into.beast.boots

Nearest railway station: Ipswich – five miles away

Capacity: 1,000

Record crowd: 550 v Ipswich Town, Suffolk Premier Cup 2006/07

Admission price: £10

Car parking: At ground

Club shop: Yes

Refreshments: Yes   **Bar:** Yes

Programme: £3

🌐 *ipswichwanderers.co.uk*

f */IpswichWanderersFC*

X *@_IWFC*

Ipswich Wanderers

League history: Ipswich Sunday League 1982-88; Eastern Counties League 1988-23; Isthmian League 2023-date

Major honours: Eastern Counties League champions 2022/3
Eastern Counties League Division One champions 1997/8, 2004/5, 21/2 (South)

Best cup runs – FA Cup: 2Q 2000/1, 01/2, 15/6
FA Trophy: 2Q 2024/5
FA Vase: Fifth round 2006/7, 15/6

Ipswich Wanderers' Humber Doucy Lane venue has been improved steadily since the club came out of Sunday football.

WELCOME TO
'THE DOUCY'

TODAY'S MATCH SPONSORS

WITH THANKS TO TODAY'S
MATCH SPONSORS

Ask behind the bar for more details
or email Sponsorship@ipswichwanderers.co.uk

IPSWICH WANDERERS FC
'Club of the Community'

Ipswich Wanderers

Mildenhall Town

Current league:
Isthmian League, North Division

Formed: 1898

Ground address: Recreation Way, Mildenhall, Bury St Edmunds, IP28 7HG

 **Centre spot reference:** truffles.tools.subjects

Nearest railway station:
Bury St Edmunds and Ely, both 14 miles

Capacity: 2,000

Record crowd: 450 v Derby County, friendly 2001/02

Admission price: £10

Car parking: Down slope at bottom of supermarket car park

Club shop: Online only

Refreshments: Yes **Bar:** Yes

Programme: £2

League history: Bury League 1945-69; Cambridgeshire League 1969-88; Eastern Counties League 1988-2017, 19-24; Isthmian League 2017-19, 24-date

Major honours: Eastern Counties League champions 2016/7, 23/4

Best cup runs – FA Cup: 3Q 2000/01
FA Trophy: 3Q 2017/8
FA Vase: Fifth round 2005/6, 06/7

www *mildenhalltownfc.com*

 *tinyurl.com/fbMildenhall*

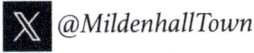 *@MildenhallTown*

Mildenhall Town played on open fields at Bridle Way and Sheldrick's Meadow before moving to the Recreation Ground.

Mildenhall Town

-48-

Newmarket Town

Current league:
Isthmian League, North Division

Formed: 1877

Ground address: Cricket Field Road, Newmarket, CB8 8BT

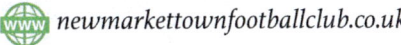 **Centre spot reference:**
member.factually.eaten

Nearest railway station:
Newmarket – seven-minute walk

Capacity: 2,750

Record crowd: 2,701 v Abbey United, FA Cup 1949/50

Admission price: £10

Car parking: At ground

Club shop: Online only

Refreshments: Yes

Bar: Yes

Programme: £2

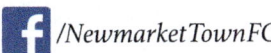 *newmarkettownfootballclub.co.uk*

/NewmarketTownFC

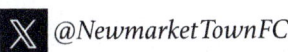 *@NewmarketTownFC*

League history: Cambridgeshire League 1919-22, 69-88; Suffolk & Ipswich League 1922-23, 28-34; United Counties League 1934-37; Bury League 1923-28, 52-56; Peterborough League 1956-59; East Anglian League; Eastern Counties League 1937-52; 59-2017, 19-24; Isthmian League 2017-19, 24-date

Major honours: Eastern Counties League Division One champions 2008/9
Suffolk & Ipswich League champions 1929/30, 33/4
Cambridgeshire League champions 1920

Best cup runs – FA Cup: 4Q 1992/3
FA Trophy: 2Q 1969/70, 2024/5
FA Vase: Quarter-final 2005/6

Welcome to the
Tristel Stadium
Home of Newmarket Town Football Club

Newmarket Town's artificial surface was installed in 2016.

Newmarket Town

Brantham Athletic is the furthest south of all Suffolk clubs, separated from Essex by the River Stour.

Current league:
Eastern Counties League, Premier Division

Formed: 1887 (Previously known as Brantham Works, Brantham Crown and Brantham & Stutton United 1995-98)

Ground address: Brantham Leisure Centre, Brantham, Cattawade, Manningtree CO11 1RZ

 Centre spot reference:
summaries.mocking.dunk

Nearest railway station:
Manningtree – 25-minute walk

Capacity: 1,200

Record crowd: 1,700 v VS Rugby, FA Vase 1982/3

Admission price: £10

Car parking: At ground

Club shop: Online only

Refreshments: Yes **Bar:** Yes

Programme: £1

 branthamathletic.com

 f /branthamathleticfc

 *@BranthamAth*

Brantham Athletic

League history: Suffolk & Ipswich League 1896-97, 98-99, 1905-7, 08-10, 12-25, 32-39, 46-50, 95-2008; SE Anglia League 1907-8, 12-14; Harwich League 1910-11; Essex & Suffolk Border League 1911-12, 25-32, 46-78; Eastern Counties League 1978-95, 2008-date

Major honours: Essex & Suffolk Border League champions 1972/3, 73/4, 75/6, 76/7

Best cup runs – FA Cup: 2Q 2018/9, 20/1
FA Vase: Fifth round 1982/3, 2012/3

Brantham Athletic

-54-

Current league:
Eastern Counties League, Premier Division

Formed: 1892

Ground address: The Millfield, Tinkers Lane, Hadleigh, IP7 5NF

 **Centre spot reference:**
gashes.jammy.tape

Nearest railway station:
Ipswich – 10 miles away

Capacity: 3,000

Record crowd: 518 v Halstead Town, FA Vase 1994/5

Admission price: £8

Car parking: At ground

Club shop: Limited

Refreshments: Yes

Bar: Yes

Programme: £1

 hadleigh-utd.co.uk

 /hadleighunitedfc

@OfficialHUFC

Hadleigh United

League history: Suffolk & Ipswich League 1929-64, 65-91; Eastern Counties League 1991-date

Major honours:
Eastern Counties League champions 2013/4
Eastern Counties League Division One champions 1993/4
Suffolk & Ipswich League champions 1953/4, 56/7, 72/3, 76/7, 78/9.

Best cup runs – FA Cup: 1Q 1995/6, 2012/3, 14/5
FA Vase: Quarter-final 2012/3

Hadleigh United's Millfield ground is tucked away on the banks of the River Brett.

Hadleigh United

Kirkley football has a long history but previous clubs have merged with Lowestoft Town. The latest incarnation has been going since 1975.

Kirkley & Pakefield

Current league:
Eastern Counties League, Premier Division

Formed: 1975 (Kirkley changed name 2007, previously known as Brooke Marine and Kirkley United)

Ground address: Walmer Road, Lowestoft, NR33 7LE

 **Centre spot reference:** ticked.picnic.heat

Nearest railway station:
Lowestoft – 45-minute walk

Capacity: 2,000

Record crowd: 1,125 v Lowestoft Town, Eastern Counties League, 2005/06

Admission price: £8

Car parking: At ground

Club shop: Yes

Refreshments: Yes **Bar:** Yes

Programme: £2

pitchero.com/clubs/kirkleypakefieldfc

tinyurl.com/fbKirkley

@KPFCOfficial

League history: Anglian Combination 1975-2003; Eastern Counties League 2007-date

Major honours: Anglian Combination champions 1999/2000, 2001/2, 02/3

Best cup runs: FA Cup: 2Q 2007/8, 09/10, 15/6
FA Vase: Fourth round 2009/10, 19/20

Kirkley & Pakefield

Lakenheath

Current league:
Eastern Counties League, Premier Division

Formed: 1907

Ground address: The Nest, Back Street, Lakenheath, Brandon, IP27 9HN

 **Centre spot reference:**
trending.achieving.curiosity

Nearest railway station:
Bury St Edmunds – 15 miles away

Capacity: 2,000

Record crowd: 1,800 v Tottenham Hotspur A, Essex & Suffolk Border League 1949/50

Admission price: £8

Car parking: At ground

Club shop: Online only

Refreshments: Yes

Bar: Yes

Programme: £1

 lakenheathfc.xyz

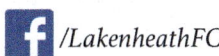 /LakenheathFC

 @Lakenheath_FC

League history: Ouse Valley League; Bury League; Essex & Suffolk Border League 1939-60; Norfolk & Suffolk League; Anglian Combination 1964-97; Cambridgeshire County League 1997-2018; Eastern Counties League 2018-date

Major honours: Cambridgeshire County League, Premier Division champions 2010/1

Best cup runs – FA Cup: Extra preliminary round 2021/2, 22/3, 23/4, 24/5
FA Vase: Fourth round: 2021/2

The Nest has been home to Lakenheath since the 1940s and is a former chalk quarry.

Lakenheath

Ipswich Town turned down a challenge to play Long Melford during the 1887/8 season because it would be 'injurious to their prestige to play little village teams'. Ironically, the teams were drawn to play each other later that season in the Suffolk Senior Cup semi-final – the 'little village' won!

Long Melford

Current league:
Eastern Counties League, Premier Division

Formed: 1868
(Merged with Melford Rovers 1936)

Ground address: Stoneylands, New Road, Long Melford, Sudbury, CO10 9JZ

 Centre spot reference:
lazy.curl.grapevine

Nearest railway station:
Sudbury – three-and-a-half miles away

Capacity: 1,000

Record crowd: 2,000 v Sudbury, early 1900s

Admission price: £8

Car parking: At ground

Club shop: Online only

Refreshments: Yes

Bar: Yes

Programme: Free

 longmelfordfc.com

 /longmelfordfc

 @Longmelfordfc

League history: Haverhill League;
Suffolk & Ipswich League 1934-6, 47-49;
Bury League; Halstead League;
Essex & Suffolk Border League 1949-2002;
Eastern Counties League 2002-date

Major honours: Eastern Counties League,
Division One champions 2014/5
Essex & Suffolk Border League champions 1954/5,
55/6, 56/7, 58/9, 60/1

Best cup runs – FA Cup: 2Q 2004/5
FA Vase: Third round 2004/5

Long Melford

Stowmarket Town

Current league:
Eastern Counties League, Premier Division

Formed: 1883 (Formed as Stowmarket Association FC by merger of Stowmarket St Peter and Stowmarket Ironworks. Added Town suffix in 1983. Also known as Stowmarket Corinthians 1947-50)

Ground address: Greens Meadow, Bury Road, Stowmarket, IP14 1JQ

 Centre spot reference: providing.visual.vampire

Nearest railway station:
Stowmarket – 15-minute walk

Capacity: 1,343

Record crowd: 1,200 v Ipswich Town, friendly 1994/5 (3,338 at Cricket Meadow, v Romford, FA Amateur Cup 1951/52

Admission price: £9

Car parking: At ground and nearby streets

Club shop: Yes   **Refreshments:** Yes   **Bar:** Yes

Programme: Online only

 stowmarkettownfc.co.uk

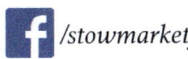 /stowmarketfc

 @stowtownfc

League history: Suffolk & Ipswich League 1896-25; Essex & Suffolk Border League 1925-38, 46-52; Eastern Counties League 1952-2021, 24-date; Isthmian League 2021-24

Major honours: Eastern Counties League Division One champions 2016/17
Suffolk & Ipswich League champions 1896/7, 97/8, 99/1900, 1907/8, 09/10, 12/13, 13/14, 21/2
Essex & Suffolk Border League champions 1950/1

Best cup runs – FA Cup: 4Q 1992/3
FA Trophy: 2Q 1969/70, 2024/5
FA Vase: Quarter-final 2005/6

Stowmarket moved into Greens Meadow in 1984.

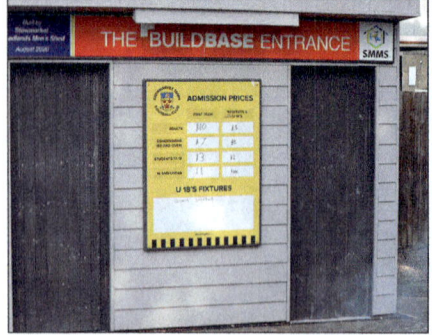

Stowmarket Town

During World War Two, Walsham's ground was ploughed up to grow food and was not returned to sporting use until 1951.

Walsham-le-Willows

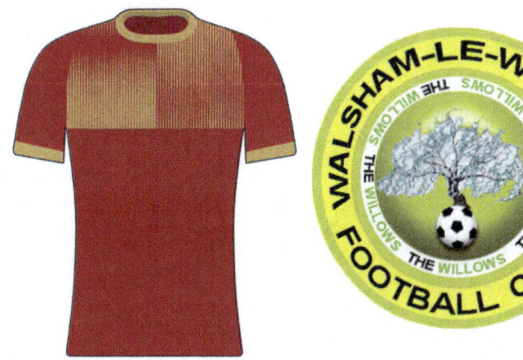

Current league:
Eastern Counties League, Premier Division

Formed: 1890

Ground address: The Meadow, Summer Road, Walsham-le-Willows, Bury St Edmunds, IP31 3AH

Centre spot reference: nudge.promotion.glitz

Nearest railway station: Bury St Edmunds – 12 miles away

Capacity: 1,200

Record crowd: 753 v Ipswich Town, Suffolk County FA Premier Cup 2012/3

Admission price: £8

Car parking: At ground

Club shop: Limited stock

Refreshments: Yes   **Bar:** Yes

Programme: £1

 walshamsportsclub.co.uk

 tinyurl.com/faceWalsham

 @Walsham_Warbler

League history: Bury League 1907-89; Suffolk & Ipswich League 1989-2004; Eastern Counties League 2004-date

Major honours: Eastern Counties League Division One champions 2006/7
Suffolk & Ipswich League champions 2001/2, 02/3

Best cup runs: FA Cup: Preliminary round 2007/8, 08/9, 11/12, 21/2
FA Vase: Fourth round 2023/4

Walsham-le-Willows

Current league:
Eastern Counties League, Premier Division

Formed: 1885 (also known as Woodbridge Old St Mary's, Woodbridge Old Comrades, Woodbridge United and Woodbridge Athletic. Woodbridge Town since 1969 –and previously 1923-36 and 1947-48)

Ground address: Notcutts Park, Fynn Road, Martlesham, Woodbridge, IP12 4LS

 Centre spot reference: encoded.dentures.putter

Nearest railway station:
Woodbridge – 30-minute walk

Capacity: 3,000

Record crowd: 3,000 v Arsenal, friendly 1990/91

Admission price: £8

Car parking: At ground

Club shop: Limited stock

Refreshments: Yes **Bar:** Yes
Programme: £1.50

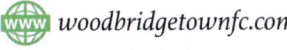 *woodbridgetownfc.com*

 */Woodbridgetown*

 *@Woodbridgetown*

Woodbridge Town

League history: Suffolk & Ipswich League 1896-1901, 1902-06, 07-14, 21-39, 46-57, 62-89; Woodbridge League; Leiston League; Eastern Counties League 1989-date

Major honours: Eastern Counties League Division One champions 2017/8
Suffolk & Ipswich League champions 1898/9, 1912/3, 88/9

Best cup runs – FA Cup: 3Q 1997/8, 2000/01
FA Vase: Quarter-final 1998/9

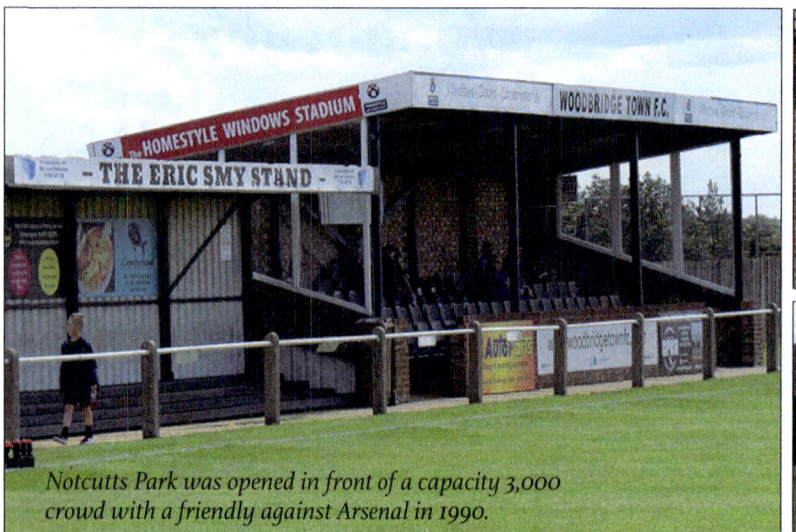

Notcutts Park was opened in front of a capacity 3,000 crowd with a friendly against Arsenal in 1990.

Woodbridge Town

Current league:
Eastern Counties League, Division One North

Formed: 1999 (an amalgamation of Sudbury Town, 1885, and Sudbury Wanderers, 1958)

Ground address: Brundon Ln, Sudbury, CO10 7HN

Centre spot reference:
universes.weddings.maddening

Nearest railway station:
Sudbury – 30-minute walk

Capacity: 2,500

Record crowd: No record kept for Reserves.

Admission price: £6

Car parking: At ground

Club shop: Limited stock

Refreshments: Yes

Bar: Yes

Programme: Online only

afcsudbury.co.uk

/AFCSudburyOfficial

@AFCSudbury

AFC Sudbury Reserves

More ground pictures are on the first-team pages – 20-23.

Current league:
Eastern Counties League, Premier Division

Formed: 1964

Ground address: Blackhouse Lane, Little Cornard, Sudbury, CO10 0NL

 Centre spot reference: carefully.apples.trouser

Nearest railway station:
Sudbury – 35-minute walk

Capacity: 2,500

Record crowd: 450 v West Ham United, friendly 2001/2

Admission price: £8

Car parking: Car park near ground

Club shop: None

Refreshments: Yes

Bar: Yes

Programme: Online only

 *cornardunited.co.uk*

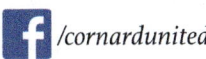 */cornardunited*

 *@CornardUtdFC*

Cornard United

League history: Sudbury Sunday League 1964-66; Bury League 1966-70; Colchester League 1970-76; Essex & Suffolk Border League 1976-89; Eastern Counties League 1989-date

Major honours: Eastern Counties League Division One champions 1989/90
Essex & Suffolk Border League champions 1988/9

Best cup runs – FA Cup: 1Q 1993/4, 94/5, 2004/5, 08/9, 24/5

FA Vase: Second round: 2008/9, 21/2

Cornard United had to rotate their pitch to enable the ground to be separated from the adjoining cricket field in order to join the Eastern Counties League in 1989.

ENTRANCE

WELCOME TO
BLACKHOUSE LANE
HOME OF THE #ARDS

NEXT HOME FIXTURE V

SPONSORED BY
VINYL VISION
GRAPHICS

Cornard United

Welcome to
Badingham Road

First Team Admission Fee's
Adults £6 Concessions £4
U16's £1 U5's Free

**Reserves & U18's Team
Admission Fee's**
Adults £3 Concessions £2
U16's £1 U5's Free

Season Tickets Available

www.thecastlemen.com

WELCOME TO

Supported by
Premier League

Making a stadium
to be proud of

NO DOGS ALLOWED
.ON THIS GROUND.

Framlingham Town

-80-

Framlingham Town

Current league:
Eastern Counties League, Division One North

Formed: 1887

Ground address: Badingham Road, Framlingham, Woodbridge, IP13 9HS

/// **Centre spot reference:**
hikes.courtyard.proof

Nearest railway station:
Saxmundham – seven miles away

Capacity: c2,000

Record crowd: c1,700 friendly
v Ipswich Town, early 2000s

Admission price: £6

Car parking: At ground

Club shop: Online only

Refreshments: Yes   **Bar:** Yes

Programme: Free with entry

 *thecastlemen.com*

 */FramTown1887*

 *@TheCastlemen*

League history: Framlingham League; Suffolk & Ipswich League 1904-5, 38-9, 66-2016; Woodbridge League; Leiston League 1945-66; Eastern Counties League 2016-date

Major honours: Suffolk & Ipswich League champions 1991/2

Best cup runs – FA Cup: Preliminary round 2017/8, 19/20

FA Vase: Second round 2017/8

A lack of floodlights prevented Framlingham Town from joining the Eastern Counties League in 1991. It took another 25 years for them to earn their place.

Framlingham Town

Haverhill Borough

Current league:
Eastern Counties League, Division One North

Formed: 2011 as Haverhill Sports Association, changed name 2013

Ground address: The New Croft 3G Arena, Chalkstone Way, Haverhill, CB9 0BW

 **Centre spot reference:**
foods.insured.buzzards

Nearest railway station:
Sudbury – 17 miles away
Cambridge – 18 miles away

Capacity: c800

Record crowd: 654 v Haverhill Rovers, FA Vase, 2016/7

Admission price: £7

Car parking: Pay & display at ground

Club shop: No

Refreshments: Yes   **Bar:** Yes

Programme: No information supplied

🌐 *tinyurl.com/webHavBoro*

f */haverhill.boroughfc*

X *@HB_FC*

League history:
Essex & Suffolk Border League 2011-13;
Eastern Counties League 2013-date

Major honours: None

Best cup runs – FA Cup: 1Q 2014/5, 17/8
FA Vase: Third round 2012/3

Haverhill Borough share the dual-surface New Croft facilities with Haverhill Rovers.

Haverhill Borough

Haverhill Rovers moved from Hamlet Croft, their home since 1913, to the New Croft in 2010.

Haverhill Rovers

Current league:
Eastern Counties League, Division One North

Formed: 1886

Ground address: The New Croft, Chalkstone Way, Haverhill, CB9 0BW

 Centre spot reference:
foods.insured.buzzards

Nearest railway station:
Sudbury – 17 miles away
Cambridge – 18 miles away

Capacity: 3,000

Record crowd: 603 v Haverhill Borough, FA Cup, 2018/19. (1,730 v Aldershot Town, FA Cup 2006/07 at Hamlet Croft)

Admission price: £7

Car parking: Pay & display at ground

Club shop: No

Refreshments: Yes   **Bar:** Yes

Programme: Online only

 tinyurl.com/webHavRov

 tinyurl.com/fbHavRov

𝕏 *@HaverhillRovers*

League history: West Suffolk League; Haverhill League; South East Anglia League; East Anglian League; Cambridge League; Halstead League; Bury League until 1912; Essex & Suffolk Border League 1912-31, 1935-64; North Essex League 1931-35; Eastern Counties League 1964-date

Major honours: Eastern Counties League champions 2013/4.
Eastern Counties League Division One champions 1993/4.
Suffolk & Ipswich League champions 1953/4, 56/7, 72/3, 76/7, 78/9

Best cup runs – FA Cup: 1Q 1995/6, 2012/3, 14/5
FA Vase: Quarter-final 2012/3

Haverhill Rovers

Leiston u23

Current league:
Eastern Counties League, Division One North

Formed: 1880 (known as Leiston Works Athletic 1919-35)

Ground address: Town Athletic Association, Victory Road, Leiston, IP16 4DQ

Centre spot reference:
inflict.innocence.envy

Nearest railway station:
Saxmundham – five miles away

Capacity: 2,250

Record crowd: 110 v Framlingham Town, Eastern Counties League 2023/4

Admission price: £5

Car parking: At ground and nearby streets

Club shop: Yes

Refreshments: Yes

Bar: Yes

Programme: Online only

🌐 *leistonfc.co.uk*

f */LeistonFootballClub*

𝕏 *@leistonfc*

More ground pictures are on the first-team pages – 24-27.

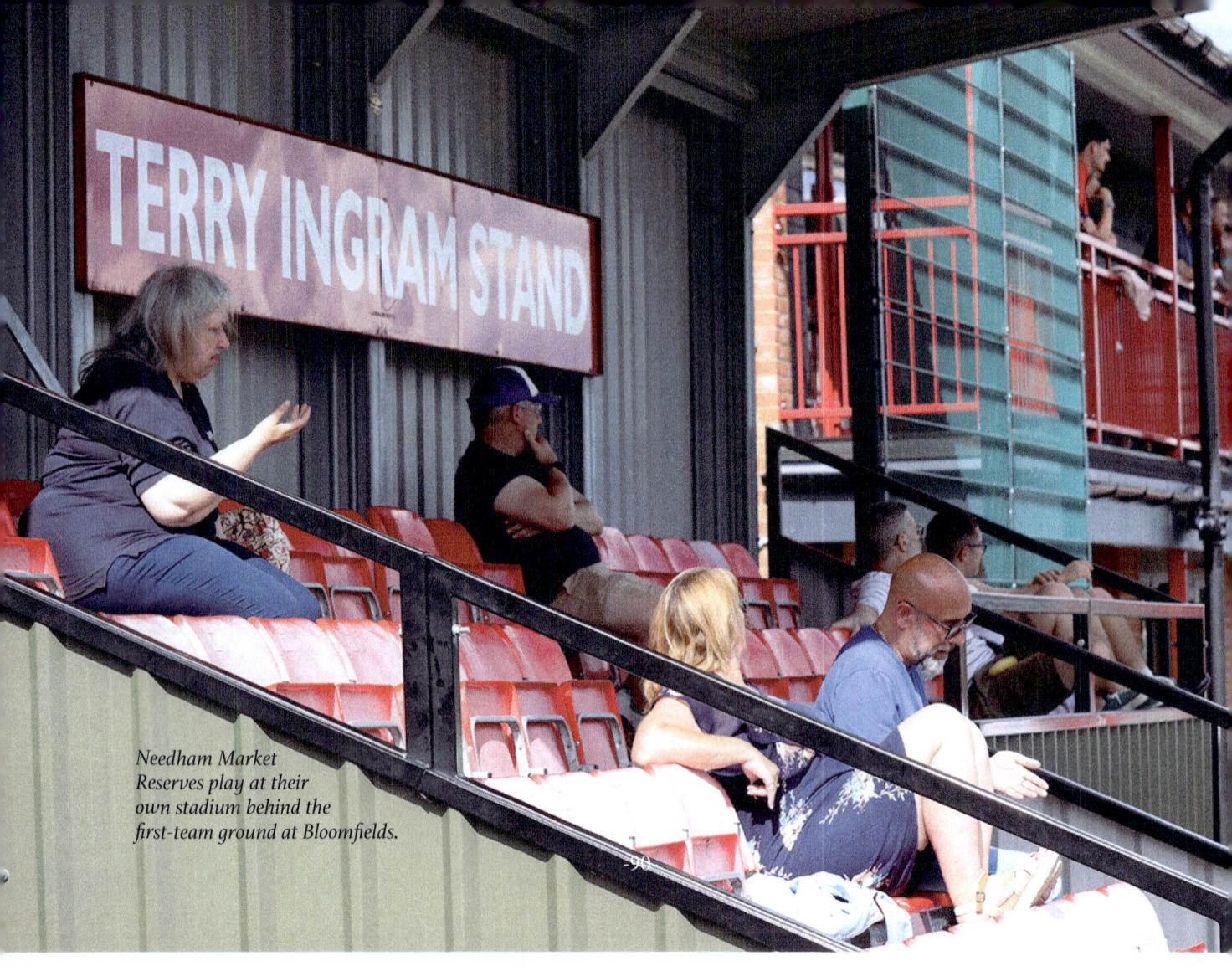

Needham Market Reserves play at their own stadium behind the first-team ground at Bloomfields.

Current league:
Eastern Counties League, Division One North

Formed: 1919

Ground address: Bloomfields 3G Arena, Quinton Rd, Needham Mkt, Ipswich, IP6 8DA

 Centre spot reference: guidebook.sample.decrease

Nearest railway station: Needham Market – 10-minute walk

Capacity: 300

Record crowd: 156 v AFC Sudbury Reserves, Eastern Counties League 2018/9

Admission price: £7

Car parking: Large car park at ground

Club shop: Yes

Refreshments: Yes

Bar: Yes

Programme: Online only

 needhammarketfc.co.uk

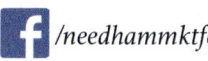 */needhammktfc*

 *@needhammktfc*

Needham Mkt Reserves

Needham Market Reserves

Needham Market Reserves share their facilities with the club's women's team and academy.

Whitton United

Current league:
Eastern Counties League, Division One North

Formed: 1926

Ground address: King George V PF, Old Norwich Road, Ipswich, IP1 6LE

 **Centre spot reference:**
gear.help.sank

Nearest railway station:
Ipswich – three miles away

Capacity: 1,000

Record crowd: 528 v Ipswich Town, friendly 1995/6

Admission price: £7 (2023/24)

Car parking: At ground

Club shop: Limited stock

Refreshments: Yes

Bar: Yes

Programme: £1

 *whittonutd.co.uk*

 *tinyurl.com/fbWhitton*

@WhittonUnitedFC

League history: Suffolk & Ipswich League 1946-71, 82-95; Essex & Suffolk Border League 1971-82; Eastern Counties League 1995-date

Major honours: Eastern Counties League Division One champions 2013/14
Suffolk & Ipswich League champions 1946/7, 47/8, 65/6, 67/8, 92/3, 94/5

Best cup runs – FA Cup: 2Q 1951/2, 53/4, 57/8, 58/9
FA Vase: Second round 2010/1, 11/2

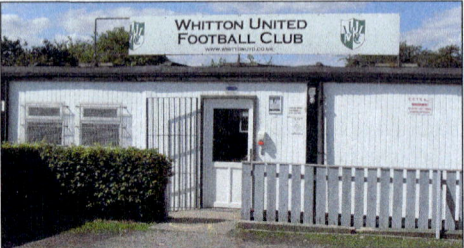

Whitton United's previous grounds were behind the Crown Inn and Maypole pub. Pint anyone?

Whitton United

Beccles Town have an impressive set-up that would not look out of place at a higher level. It is also extremely handy for the railway station.

Beccles Town

Current league:
Anglian Combination, Premier Division

Formed: 1919 (as Beccles FC)

Ground address: College Meadow, Common Lane South, Beccles, NR34 9BU

 Centre spot reference:
typed.earplugs.unrealistic

Nearest railway station:
Beccles – five-minute walk

Capacity: c400

Record crowd: c3,000 Suffolk Premier Cup semi-final 1955/6 – Bungay Tn v Lowestoft Tn.

Admission price: £4

Car parking: At ground

Club shop: Online only

Refreshments: Yes

Bar: Yes

Programme: Free with entry

 becclestownfc.org.uk

 /becclestownfcinfo

@BecclesFC

League history: Norfolk & Suffolk League 1919-32; 49-64; East Anglian League 1932-61; Anglian Combination 1964-date

Major honours: Norfolk & Suffolk League champions 1952/3

Best cup runs – FA Cup: 3Q 1952/3, 1954/5, 1955/6
FA Vase: First round 1978/9

Bungay Town's Maltings Meadow ground is on the 'wrong' side of the River Waveney, across the county border in Norfolk.

BUNGAY TOWN FC

ENTRANCE FEE: £3

CONCESSIONS: £2
(SENIOR CITIZENS & CHILDREN)

Bungay Town

Current league:
Anglian Combination, Premier Division

Formed: 1925 (merger of Bungay United and Bungay Harriers)

Ground address: Maltings Meadow, Pirnhow Street, Bungay, NR35 2RU

 **Centre spot reference:**
scramble.packets.mixing

Nearest railway station:
Beccles – six miles away

Capacity: c1,000

Record crowd: 1,618 v Great Yarmouth Town, FA Cup 1956/7 (2,498 at Recreation Ground v Wycombe Wanderers, FA Amateur Cup 1949/50)

Admission price: £4

Car parking: At ground

Club shop: No

Refreshments: Yes **Bar:** Yes

Programme: Free

 bungaytownfc.org.uk

 tinyurl.com/fbBungayTn

✕ @BungayTownFC

League history: Lowestoft League, North Suffolk League, East Anglian League 1926-33, Norwich League 1933-35; Norfolk & Suffolk League 1935-63; Eastern Counties League 1963-64; Anglian Combination 1964-date

Major honours: Norfolk & Suffolk League champions 1946/7, 47/8, 48/9, 51/2

Best cup runs – FA Cup: 3Q 1956/7, 59/60, 60/1
FA Vase: First round: 1974/5, 75/6, 76/7, 79/80, 81/2

Waveney will be developing their Saturn Close venue after securing a longer lease.

SATURN CLOSE HOME OF WAVENEY F.C.

NO PARKING AMBULANCE ACCESS

Waveney

Current league:
Anglian Combination, Premier Division

Formed: 1978

Ground address: Saturn Close, Lowestoft, NR32 4TE

 **Centre spot reference:** dress.shin.list

Nearest railway station:
Lowestoft – 30-minute walk

Capacity: c400

Record crowd: Not recorded

Admission price: Free

Car parking: At ground

Club shop: Online only

Refreshments: Yes

Bar: No

Programme: No

🌐 *tinyurl.com/webWaveney*

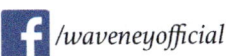 */waveneyofficial*

 *@waveneyofficial*

The United's Kingdom's furthest east corner flag flutters proudly at Waveney FC in Lowestoft. It is nearer to the Netherlands than it is to London, Luton or Lincoln.

Bacton moved from St Mary's to a new ground at Brickwall Meadow thanks to Football Foundation support.

Pictures: courtesy Bacton United '89.

Current league:
Suffolk & Ipswich League, Senior Division

Formed: 1989

Ground address: Brickwall Meadow,
Broad Lane, Bacton, Stowmarket, IP14 4HR

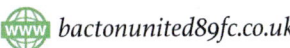 **Centre spot reference:**
balance.glider.companies

Nearest railway station:
Stowmarket – six miles away

Capacity: c400

Record crowd: Not recorded

Admission price: Free

Car parking: At ground

Club shop: No

Refreshments: Yes

Bar: Yes

Programme: No

 *bactonunited89fc.co.uk*

 */BactonUnited89FC*

@BactonUnited89

Bacton United '89

The Ipswich School Sports Centre pitches are shared with AFC Kesgrave.

Coplestonians

Current league:
Suffolk & Ipswich League, Senior Division

Formed: 1973

Ground address: Ipswich School Sports Cen, The Street, Rushmere St Andrew, IP5 1DE

 Centre spot reference: cats.boats.deal

Nearest railway station:
Ipswich – five miles away

Capacity: c400

Record crowd: Not recorded

Admission price: Free

Car parking: At ground

Club shop: No

Refreshments: No

Bar: No

Programme: No

 *coplestoniansfc.org*

 *tinyurl.com/fbCoples*

 *@Cops_FC*

Coplestonians were playing at the SEH Ground during the 2023/24 season – both at Ipswich Wanderers (see pages 40-43) and the back pitch.

Debenham Leisure Centre, to give the club its full title, enjoyed an 18-year stint in the Eastern Counties League.

Debenham LC

Current league:
Suffolk & Ipswich League, Senior Division

Formed: 1991 as Debenham Angels (became AFC Debenham in 1994 and Debenham Leisure Centre in 2005)

Ground address: Friends' Meadow, Gracechurch Street, Debenham, Stowmarket, IP14 6BL

 **Centre spot reference:** cyber.paddock.blaring

Nearest railway station:
Stowmarket – nine miles away

Capacity: c700

Record crowd: 1,026 v AFC Wimbledon, FA Cup 2007/8

Admission price: Free

Car parking: At ground

Club shop: No   **Refreshments:** Yes   **Bar:** Yes

Programme: No

 debenhamlcfc.co.uk

 /debenhamLCFC

 @DebenhamLCFC

League history: Suffolk & Ipswich League 1991-2005, 2023-date;
Eastern Counties League 2005-2023

Major honours: None

Best cup runs – FA Cup: 2Q 2007/8
FA Vase: Second round 2008/9

An arresting sight: East Bergholt play in the heart of Constable Country on the Essex/Suffolk border.

East Bergholt United

Current league:
Suffolk & Ipswich League, Senior Division

Formed: 1895

Ground address: Gandish Road PF,
East Bergholt, Colchester, CO7 6TP

 Centre spot reference:
surpassed.agents.differ

Nearest railway station:
Manningtree – three miles away

Capacity: c400

Record crowd: Not recorded

Admission price: Free

Car parking: At ground

Club shop: No

Refreshments: Yes

Bar: Yes

Programme: Occasionally, free

 eastbergholtunited.com

 /EastBergholtUnitedFootballClub

@EBUFC1

Grundisburgh returned to senior football for the 2024/25 season after five years in Division One of the Suffolk & Ipswich League.

Grundisburgh

Current league:
Suffolk & Ipswich League, Senior Division

Formed: 1920

Ground address: Ipswich Road PF, Grundisburgh, Woodbridge,

 Centre spot reference:
legal.face.soda

Nearest railway station:
Woodbridge – four miles

Capacity: c400

Record crowd: Not recorded

Admission price: Free

Car parking: At ground

Club shop: No

Refreshments: Yes

Bar: Yes

Programme: No

 *None*

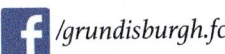 */grundisburgh.fc*

 *@FcGrundisburgh*

INARDUIS VIGET VIRTUS

*Halesworth Town have
been in the Suffolk &
Ipswich League since 1966.*

Halesworth Town

Current league:
Suffolk & Ipswich League, Senior Division

Formed: 1887

Ground address: Dairy Hill,
Halesworth, IP19 8JS

 **Centre spot reference:**
intruding.grapes.clinking

Nearest railway station:
Halesworth – five-minute walk

Capacity: c400

Record crowd: Not recorded

Admission price: Donation collection

Car parking: At ground

Club shop: No

Refreshments: Yes

Bar: Yes

Programme: No

 *None*

 tinyurl.com/fbHales

@HalesworthClub

Haughley United boast some top-class off-field facilities.

Haughley United

Current league:
Suffolk & Ipswich League, Senior Division

Formed: 1898

Ground address: King George V PF,
Green Road, Haughley, Stowmarket, IP14 3RA

 **Centre spot reference:**
grudging.utensil.rinse

Nearest railway station:
Stowmarket – three miles away

Capacity: c400

Record crowd: Not recorded

Admission price: Free

Car parking: At ground

Club shop: Yes

Refreshments: Yes

Bar: Yes

Programme: No

Old Pitchero only

No current one

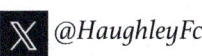 *@HaughleyFc*

Henley Athletic are on a run of three consecutive Suffolk & Ipswich League titles and also won in 2017.

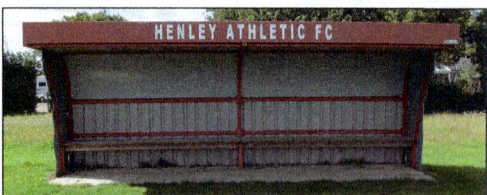

Henley Athletic

Current league:
Suffolk & Ipswich League, Senior Division

Formed: 1991 (as Orwell Athletic. Changed to current name in 2003)

Ground address: Church Meadows, Henley, Ipswich, IP6 0RP

Centre spot reference: cuts.square.resist

Nearest railway station:
Ipswich – six miles away

Capacity: c400

Record crowd: 305 v Ipswich Town u18s, Suffolk County FA Senior Cup, 2019/20

Admission price: Free

Car parking: At ground

Club shop: No

Refreshments: No

Bar: Yes

Programme: £2

 *henleyathleticfc.co.uk*

 *tinyurl.com/fbHens*

 *@HenleyAFC*

Leiston St Margaret's have been members of the Suffolk & Ipswich League since 1953.

Leiston St Margaret's

Current league:
Suffolk & Ipswich League, Senior Division

Formed: 1895

Ground address: Junction Meadow, Abbey Road, Leiston, IP16 4RD

 **Centre spot reference:** broom.clerk.threaded

Nearest railway station: Saxmundham – four miles away

Capacity: c400

Record crowd: Not recorded

Admission price: Free

Car parking: At ground

Club shop: Online only

Refreshments: Yes

Bar: Yes

Programme: No

None

 *tinyurl.com/fbLSMarg*

 *@LSMFC*

Old Newton's first ground was at Hill Farm, where players had to shoo away the cows before they could play.

Old Newton United

Current league:
Suffolk & Ipswich League, Senior Division

Formed: 1959

Ground address: Church Road PF,
Old Newton, Stowmarket, IP14 4ED

 Centre spot reference:
talker.vans.fictional

Nearest railway station:
Stowmarket – three miles away

Capacity: c400

Record crowd: Not recorded

Admission price: Free

Car parking: At ground

Club shop: No

Refreshments: Yes

Bar: Yes

Programme: No

 Old Pitchero only

 tinyurl.com/fbONU

 @OldNewtonUnited

Sporting '87 have about 30 youth teams, from u7s to u18s, along with several girls-only teams.

Current league:
Suffolk & Ipswich League, Senior Division

Formed: 1987

Ground address: Victory Sports Ground,
Nowton Road, Bury St Edmunds, IP33 2BT

 Centre spot reference:
boost.traps.innovator

Nearest railway station:
Bury St Edmunds – 45-minute walk

Capacity: c500

Record crowd: Not recorded

Admission price: Free

Car parking: At ground

Club shop: No

Refreshments: Yes

Bar: Yes

Programme: Yes, free

 sporting87fc.co.uk

 *None*

@Official_S87

Sporting '87

Stowupland Falcons moved to their present ground in 1990. Their previous Village Green venue was often interrupted by villagers crossing the pitch on their bicycles.

Stowupland Falcons

Current league:
Suffolk & Ipswich League, Senior Division

Formed: 1901 (also known as Stowupland, Stowupland Swifts and Stowupland Corinthians

Ground address: Church Road PF, Stowupland, Stowmarket, IP14 4BG

Centre spot reference: whisker.reckon.scarred

Nearest railway station: Stowmarket – 35-minute walk

Capacity: c400

Record crowd: Not recorded

Admission price: Free

Car parking: At ground

Club shop: Online only

Refreshments: Yes

Bar: Yes

Programme: None

 *stowuplandfalconsfc.co.uk*

 *tinyurl.com/fbStowFalc*

 *@StowFalcons*

Tattingstone United are playing at the Bourne Vale Sports Club in Ipswich until they are able to bring the idyllic Green Lane ground in their home village up to standard.

Tattingstone United

Current league:
Suffolk & Ipswich League, Senior Division

Formed: 1965

Ground address: Bourne Vale Sports Club, Halifax Road, Ipswich, IP2 8RE

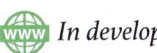 **Centre spot reference:** deduct.guises.plump

Nearest railway station: Ipswich – 30-minute walk

Capacity: c400

Record crowd: 200 v Trimley Red Devils, Morrison Freight semi-final 2023/4

Admission price: Free (donations welcome)

Car parking: At ground

Club shop: No

Refreshments: Yes **Bar:** Yes

Programme: No

In development

 */TattingstoneUtd*

 *@Tattingstoneutd*

Trimley Red Devils were formed in 1975 with a single team of boys varying in age from nine to 11.

Trimley Red Devils

Current league:
Suffolk & Ipswich League, Senior Division

Formed: 1975

Ground address: Stennetts Playing Field, Trimley St Mary, Felixstowe, IP11 0TZ

 **Centre spot reference:**
mats.breeze.toolkit

Nearest railway station:
Felixstowe – 40-minute walk

Capacity: c400

Record crowd: Not recorded

Admission price: Free

Car parking: At ground

Club shop: No

Refreshments: Yes

Bar: No

Programme: No

trdfc.co.uk

 */TrimleyRedDevilsFC*

 *@TrimRedDevils*

Wickham Market joined the
Suffolk & Ipswich League in 1970,
42 years after they were formed.

Wickham Market

Current league:
Suffolk & Ipswich League, Senior Division

Formed: 1928

Ground address: Village Hall PF, High Street, Wickham Market, Woodbridge IP13 0HE

 **Centre spot reference:**
late.compliant.trooper

Nearest railway station:
Wickham Market – 50-minute walk

Capacity: c400

Record crowd: No record kept

Admission price: Free

Car parking: At ground

Club shop: No

Refreshments: Yes

Bar: Yes

Programme: No

 *None*

 */WickhamMarketFC*

 *@WickhamMarketFC*

Current league:
Cambridgeshire League, Premier Division

Formed: 1877

Ground address: Cricket Field Road,
Newmarket, CB8 8BT

 Centre spot reference:
member.factually.eaten

Nearest railway station:
Newmarket – seven-minute walk

Capacity: 2,750

Record crowd: No records kept

Admission price: Free

Car parking: At ground

Club shop: Online only

Refreshments: Yes

Bar: Yes

Programme: No

🌐 *newmarkettownfootballclub.co.uk*

 */NewmarketTownFC*

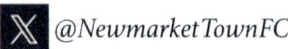 *@NewmarketTownFC*

Newmarket Tn Reserves

**More ground pictures are on the first-team pages
– 48-51.**

Kings Park Rangers

Current league:
Essex & Suffolk Border League,
Premier Division

Formed: 2023

Ground address: Blackhouse Lane,
Little Cornard, Sudbury, CO10 0NL

 **Centre spot reference:**
carefully.apples.trouser

Nearest railway station:
Sudbury – 35-minute walk

Capacity: 2,500

Record crowd: 423 v East Thurrock,
Essex & Suffolk Border League, 2024/5

Admission price: Free

Car parking: Public car park near ground

Club shop: Planned

Refreshments: Yes

Bar: Yes

Programme: No

 *linktr.ee/kingsparkrfc*

tinyurl.com/KPRFace

@KingsParkRFC

**More ground pictures are on the Cornard United
pages – 77-79.**

Sudbury Sports

Current league:
Essex & Suffolk Border League, Premier Division

Formed: 2017 (previously AFC Sudbury 'A')

Ground address: Brundon Lane, Sudbury, CO10 7HN

 Centre spot reference: universes.weddings.maddening

Nearest railway station:
Sudbury – 30-minute walk

Capacity: 2,500

Record crowd: Not recorded

Admission price: £4

Car parking: At ground

Club shop: No

Refreshments: Yes

Bar: Yes

Programme: No

 None

 None

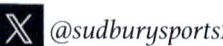 *@sudburysports1*

More ground pictures are on the AFC Sudbury pages – 20-23.

Current league:
Anglian Combination, Division One

Formed: 1975 (Kirkley changed name 2007, previously known as Brooke Marine and Kirkley United)

 Ground address: Walmer Road, Lowestoft, NR33 7LE

Centre spot reference:
ticked.picnic.heat

Nearest railway station:
Lowestoft – 45-minute walk

Capacity: 2,000

Record crowd: Not recorded

Admission price: £5

Car parking: At ground

Club shop: Yes

Refreshments: Yes **Bar:** Yes

Programme: No

 pitchero.com/clubs/kirkleypakefieldfc

tinyurl.com/fbKirkley

 *@KPFCOfficial*

Kirkley/Pakefield Res

More ground pictures are on the first-team pages – 58-60.

Brandon Town's major derby rivals used to be Brandon Tip (Town Street).

Brandon Town

Current league:
Anglian Combination, Division One

Formed: 1904

Ground address: Remembrance PF, Church Road, Brandon, IP27 0JB

 **Centre spot reference:** acted.lifestyle.liners

Nearest railway station: Brandon – 20-minute walk

Capacity: c400

Record crowd: Not recorded

Admission price: Free

Car parking: At ground

Club shop: No

Refreshments: Yes

Bar: Yes

Programme: No

 *brandontownfc.co.uk*

 */brandontownfootballclub*

@BrandonTownFC

Mutford & Wrentham have enjoyed a remarkable rise through the junior ranks from the Lowestoft League to Division One of the Anglian Combination.

Current league:
Anglian Combination, Division One

Formed: 1880 (at current ground since 1920)

Ground address: London Road, Wrentham, Beccles, NR34 7HH

 Centre spot reference:
conspired.taxed.payout

Nearest railway station:
Beccles – Eight miles away (also Halesworth and Lowestoft, both nine miles)

Capacity: c1,000

Record crowd: Not recorded

Admission price: Free

Car parking: At ground

Club shop: No

Refreshments: Yes

Bar: No

Programme: No

🌐 *None*

f */mutfordandwrentham*

𝕏 *@MWFC_*

Mutford & Wrentham

Thetford Rovers play over the county border at Euston Hall in Suffolk, three miles south of their home town

Current league:
Anglian Combination, Division One

Formed: 1922

Ground address: Euston Park, Thetford, IP24 2QQ

 **Centre spot reference:** outwards.gasp.castle

Nearest railway station: Thetford – four miles away

Capacity: c400

Record crowd: Not recorded

Admission price: Free

Car parking: At ground

Club shop: Online only

Refreshments: Yes

Bar: No

Programme: No

🌐 *thetfordroversfc.co.uk*

 */thetfordroversfc*

 *@Thetfordrovers*

Thetford Rovers

Bildeston Rangers

Bildeston pulled out of the Suffolk & Ipswich League during the 2023/24 season.

Westerfield United

Westerfield's facilities remain in place at Ipswich School Sports Centre, despite their demise in 2023/24.

Spexhall Huntsman & Hounds

Spexhall Huntsman & Hounds pulled both their teams out of the Lowestoft & District League during the summer of 2024. The excellent facilities are still used by the club's old boys in the Norfolk & Suffolk Veterans League.

Achilles

Formed in 1937 as a merger of St Clements United and St Clements Institute, Achilles have played in both the FA Cup and FA Amateur Cup. They are currently in Division One of the Suffolk & Ipswich League and play at Pauls Sports & Social Club

AFC Kesgrave

AFC Kesgrave are playing at the Ipswich School Sports Centre in Rushmere St Andrew but plan to move to the former Hollies Sports Centre in Straight Lane, Foxhall. It has been unused for more than 20 years and will need major redevelopment work before the Suffolk & Ipswich League Division One club can move in. Hollies picture: Flickr/the_man_1984

Beccles Caxton

Beccles Caxton have an impressive record since their formation in 1880 (despite the gates at their Caxton Meadow home stating 1890). The Anglian Combination Division Two club have competed in the FA Cup and played in the FA Amateur Cup between 1899 and 1959. They dominated Suffolk football at the end of the 19th Century, sharing county cup honours with Ipswich Town.

Benhall St Mary

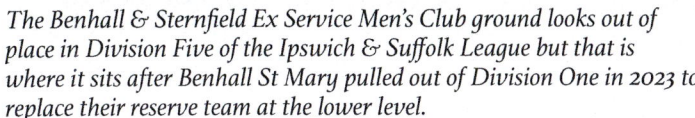

The Benhall & Sternfield Ex Service Men's Club ground looks out of place in Division Five of the Ipswich & Suffolk League but that is where it sits after Benhall St Mary pulled out of Division One in 2023 to replace their reserve team at the lower level.

Boxford Rovers

Boxford are in Division Two of the Essex & Suffolk Border League.

Bramford United

Bramford United's Acton Road ground is hosting Suffolk & Ipswich League Division Five football.

Clare Town

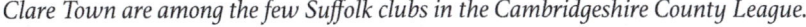

Clare Town are among the few Suffolk clubs in the Cambridgeshire County League.

Claydon

Claydon pulled out of the Suffolk & Ipswich League's Senior Division during the 2023/24 season. Their Blue Circle Ground in Great Blakenham now hosts Division Two football after they replaced their reserves.

Coddenham Athletic

Coddenham United were formed around 1900 but by 1977, when they returned to the Suffolk & Ipswich League, they were known as Coddenham Country Club. The current incarnation play in Division Three.

The Dip Farm complex is Suffolk's closest ground to the sea. It sits just a hefty clearance away from the beach, across Gunton Warren. The pitches are used by various Lowestoft League teams, Waveney FC's junior sides and for local cup finals.

Dip Farm

Hundon

Cambs League side Hundon are back in their home village after a four-year exile in Clare while a new pavilion was built at their North Street ground.

Kirton Athletic

Kirton Athletic of the Suffolk & Ipswich League play in Trimley St Martin. Picture: Google Street View.

Mendlesham play in the Suffolk & Ipswich League and also have a team in the Bury & District Sunday League

Mendlesham

Ransomes Sports

The original Ransomes were established as Orwell Works and enjoyed success at the start of the 1900s. As Ransomes they won the Suffolk Senior Cup twice before adding RSSC as a prefix, under which title they twice reached the third round of the FA Vase. That club folded in 1995 but groundless Rushmere Athletic (previously Fisons) moved into the Ransomes & Reavell Sports Club and renamed themselves Ransomes Sports.

Somersham

Somersham are in Division One of the Suffolk & Ipswich League. The village team were formed in 1968 and entered the league in 1983.

Southwold Town have played in both the Anglian Combination and Suffolk & Ipswich League but are currently in Division Three of the Lowestoft & District League at Level 19.

Southwold Town

Stanton

Stanton have played in the Suffolk & Ipswich League at their Old Bury Road Recreation Ground since 1991.

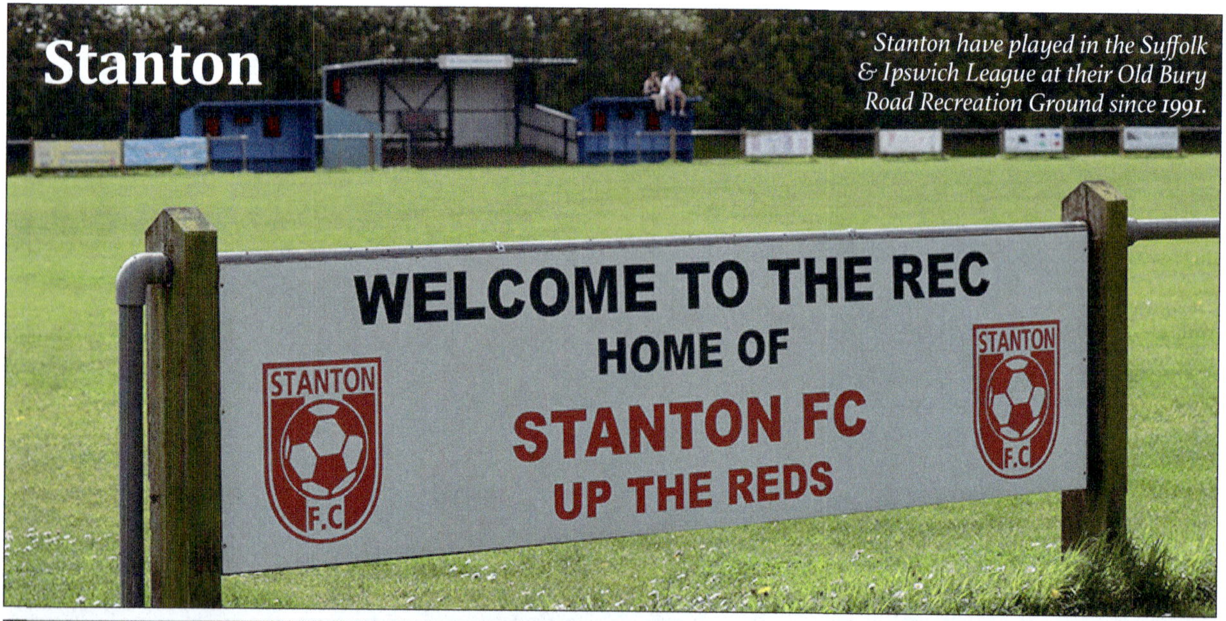

WELCOME TO THE REC
HOME OF
STANTON FC
UP THE REDS
STANTON
F.C
STANTON
F.C

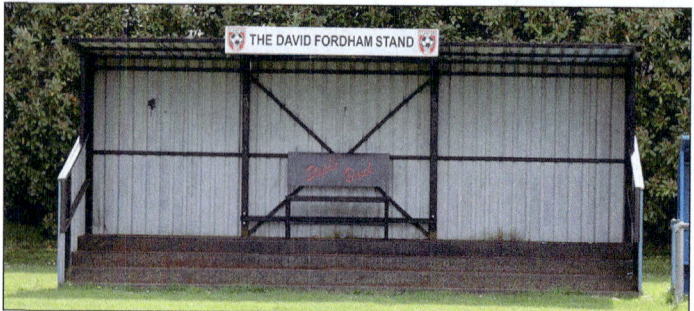

THE DAVID FORDHAM STAND

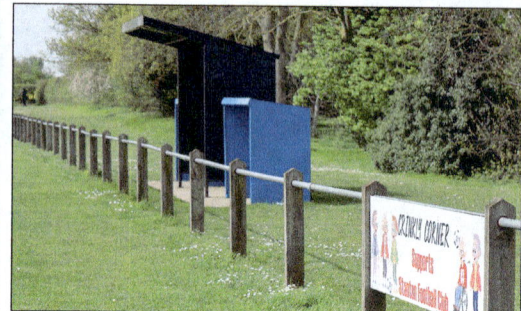

Thurlow

Cambs League side Thurlow were established in 2007 and play at the tree-lined Wratting Road Recreation Ground in Great Thurlow.

Thurston

Suffolk & Ipswich League Division One champions Thurston were denied promotion to the Senior Division in 2024 due to their ground facilities.

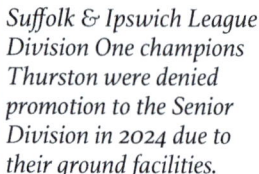

Woolverstone United

The Hazelwoods ground is noted for the ancient tree between the clubhouse and pitch. It features on the club badge and team pictures throughout the decades. The club were formed in 1921 but did not enter the Suffolk & Ipswich League until 1948.

Senior teams – the last 16 seasons

	23/4	22/3	21/2	20/1	19/0	18/9	17/8	16/7	15/6	14/5	13/4	12/3	11/2	10/1	09/10	08/9
AFC Sudbury	G18	h2	h7	hab	hab	h8	h12	g23	h1	h3	h10	h17	h8	h7	h14	h12
AFC Sudbury Res	J13	J8	J14	Jab	Jab	J13	J11	J18	J10	J14	J16	Zo6	Zs10	Zs3	Zs9	Zs6
Brantham Ath	I17	I13	I18	Iab	Iab	I8	I5	I8	I11	I8	I11	I4	I3	I13	J3	J8
Bury Town	h2	h11	h12	hab	hab	h6	h9	h11	h13	g24	g15	g7	g5	g3	H1	H7
Cornard Utd	J5	J7	J18	Jab	Jab	J12	J13	J15	J15	J18	J18	J18	J16	J17	J13	J11
Debenham LC	K10	J19	J11	Jab	Jab	J11	J7	J12	J13	J7	J12	J15	J7	I22	I14	J3
Felixstowe & WU	h3	h6	h5	hab	hab	h11	I2	I2	I4	I5	I3	I14	I18	I18	I7	I12
Felixstowe Res	-	z?	K18	Kab	Jab	J19	Z7	Z8	Z9	Zp4	Zp?	Zo2	Zs11	Zs11	Zs4	Zn6
Framlingham	J2	J3	J5	Jab	Jab	I20	J2	J7	K5	L2	L3	L10	K16	K10	K11	K7
Hadleigh Utd	I11	I9	I15	Iab	Iab	I16	I21	I18	I7	I7	I1	I8	I11	I9	I18	J2
Haverhill Boro	J20	J17	J19	Jab	Jab	J16	J20	J3	J8	J6	J4	K2	L1	-	-	-
Haverhill Rov	J10	J19	J17	Jab	Jab	I12	I19	I16	I12	I17	I7	I10	I14	I8	I12	I21
Ipswich Wdrs	h17	I1	J1	Jab	Jab	J10	I23	I10	I15	I9	J3	J4	J12	J10	J17	J17
Ipswich Town	B2	C2	C11	C9	C11	B24	B12	B16	B7	B6	B9	B14	B15	B13	B15	B9
Kirkley/Pakefield	I19	I16	I9	Iab	Iab	I5	I10	I11	I5	I4	I12	I12	I13	I12	I4	I6
Lakenheath	I10	I5	I12	Jab	Jab	J5	K8	K3	K6	K2	K5	K9	K2	K1	K3	K2
Leiston	G13	G3	G7	Gab	Gab	G19	g5	g7	g8	g9	g9	g12	h1	I1	I3	I7
Leiston u23/Res	J18	J16	J9	Jab	Jab	J9	J13	J21	J6	J19	z?	Zp9	Zn3	Zn10	Zn8	Zn14
Long Melford	I15	I11	I19	Iab	Iab	I17	I16	I17	I9	J1	J11	J13	J9	J12	J16	J19
Lowestoft Tn	h1	h3	G21	Gab	Gab	G14	g22	g11	F20	F16	g4	g2	g3	g4	h1	I1
Mildenhall Tn	I1	I6	I3	Iab	Iab	h20	h22	I1	I6	I10	I10	I7	I7	I5	I6	I11
Needham Mkt	G1	G17	G12	Gab	Gab	G11	g19	g9	g20	h1	h5	h15	h4	h2	I1	I3
Needham Res	J21	J15	J14	Jab	Jab	J17	J20	J19	J19	J16	J15	Zp4	Zn2	Zn6	Zn6	Zn8
Newmarket Tn	I2	I12	I8	Iab	Iab	I10	I9	I3	I13	I6	I9	J2	I20	I19	I16	J1
Stowmarket Tn	h19	h7	h4	Iab	Iab	I4	I3	J1	J14	J11	J14	J17	J15	J7	J15	J12
Team Bury	-	-	-	-	-	-	J21	J17	J18	J12	J10	J12	J10	J13	J9	K2
Walsham-le-Wil	I8	I14	I7	Iab	Iab	I9	I17	I14	I14	I15	I8	I6	I17	I17	I13	I10
Whitton Utd	J17	I20	I16	Iab	Iab	I13	J3	J11	I20	I11	J1	J7	J3	J2	J10	Ix
Woodbridge	I13	I4	I11	Iab	Iab	I2	J4	J9	J12	J9	J17	J6	I10	I10	I4	J18

Key: – B: Level 2 (Champ), C: 3 (FL1), D: 4 (FL2), F: 6 (Step 2, National North), G: 7 (Step 3, SL Prem), g: (IL Prem), H: 8 (Step 4, SL Div 1) h: (IL Div 1), I: 9 (Step 5, ECL Prem), J: 10 (Step 6, ECL 1), K: Level 11 (Step 7 – SIL Snr, Ang Comb Prem, Cambs Prem, Essex/Suffolk Prem), L: 12 (SIL Div 1), Z: ECL Reserve League (p, o, n, s – Premier, One, North, South, z: Isthmian Reserve/Development League.   ab: season abandoned (Covid),   x: record expunged,   –: did not compete,   ?: finishing position not known.

Major league title winners

Football League (current Premier League, Level 1)
1962 Ipswich Town

FL Division Two (current Championship, Level 2)
1961 Ipswich Town
1968 Ipswich Town
1992 Ipswich Town

FL Division Three (current League One, Level 3)
1954 Ipswich Town [Div Three South]
1957 Ipswich Town [Div Three South]

Step 3 – Southern and Isthmian Leagues Premier Divisions, Level 7
1937 Ipswich Town [SL]
2024 Needham Market [SL Prem Cen]

Step 4 – Southern and Isthmian Leagues Divisions One, Level 8
2010 Bury Town [SL Div 1 Central]
2010 Lowestoft Town [IL Division 1]
2012 Leiston [IL Division 1]
2015 Needham Market [IL Division 1]
2016 AFC Sudbury [IL Division 1]
2024 Lowestoft Town [IL North Div]

Step 5 – Eastern Counties League Premier Division, Level 9
1938 Lowestoft Town
1963 Lowestoft Town
1964 Bury Town
1965 Lowestoft Town
1966 Lowestoft Town
1967 Lowestoft Town
1968 Lowestoft Town
1970 Lowestoft Town
1971 Lowestoft Town
1974 Sudbury Town
1975 Sudbury Town
1976 Sudbury Town
1978 Lowestoft Town
1979 Haverhill Rovers
1986 Sudbury Town
1987 Sudbury Town
1989 Sudbury Town
1990 Sudbury Town
2001 AFC Sudbury
2002 AFC Sudbury
2003 AFC Sudbury
2004 AFC Sudbury
2005 AFC Sudbury
2006 Lowestoft Town
2009 Lowestoft Town
2010 Needham Market
2011 Leiston
2014 Hadleigh United
2017 Mildenhall Town
2023 Ipswich Wanderers
2024 Mildenhall Town

Step 6 – Eastern Counties League Division One, Level 10
1990 Cornard United
1993 Sudbury Wanderers
1994 Hadleigh United
1998 Ipswich Wanderers
2005 Ipswich Wanderers
2007 Walsham-le-Willows
2009 Newmarket Town
2014 Whitton United
2015 Long Melford
2017 Stowmarket Town
2018 Woodbridge Town
2022 Ipswich Wdrs [South]

Step 7, Level 11
Suffolk & Ipswich League Senior Division
(Previously Ipswich & District League)
1897 Stowmarket
1898 Stowmarket
1899 Woodbridge Old St Mary's
1900 Stowmarket
1901 Leiston
1902 Leiston
1903 Leiston
1904 28th RGA Landguard
1905 Orwell Works
1906 Orwell Works
1907 Orwell Works
1908 Stowmarket
1909 Westbourne Mills
1910 Stowmarket
1911 Felixstowe Town
1912 Orwell Works
1913* Woodbridge Tn [AFA]
1913* Stowmarket [FA]
1914* Walton United [AFA]
1914* Stowmarket [FA]

That's champion!

Suffolk & Ipswich League Senior Division (continued)

1915-19	No competition
1920	Bury United
1921	Walton United
1922	Stowmarket
1923	Harwich & Parkeston [Essex]
1924	RAF Martlesham
1925	RAF Martlesham
1926	Walton United
1927	HMS Ganges
1928	HMS Ganges
1929	Lowestoft Waveney Athletic
1930	Newmarket Town
1931	Stoke Institute
1932	RAF Martlesham
1933	Orwell Works
1934	Newmarket Town
1935	Sudbury Town
1936	Orwell Works
1937	Felixstowe Town
1938	Orwell Works
1939	Orwell Works
1940-45	No competition
1946	Achilles and HMS Ganges [joint winners]
1947	Whitton United
1948	Whitton United
1949	Achilles
1950	Waterside Works
1951	Waterside Works
1952	Waterside Works
1953	Sudbury Town
1954	Hadleigh United
1955	Waterside Works
1956	Waterside Works

1957	Hadleigh United
1958	Felixstowe Town
1959	Waterside Works
1960	Electric Supply
1961	Orwell Works
1962	Orwell Works
1963	Waterside Works
1964	Waterside Works
1965	Felixstowe Town
1966	Whitton United
1967	Electric Supply
1968	Whitton United
1969	Electric Supply
1970	ICI Paints
1971	Heath Row
1972	Nicholians
1973	Hadleigh United
1974	Nicholians
1975	Crane Sports
1976	Nicholians
1977	Hadleigh United
1978	Bull Motors
1979	Hadleigh United
1980	Nicholians
1981	Ransomes
1982	Westerfield United
1983	Haughley United
1984	Westerfield United
1985	Westerfield United
1986	Achilles
1987	RSSC Ransomes
1988	Achilles
1989	Woodbridge Town
1990	Grundisburgh
1991	Grundisburgh
1992	Framlingham Town

1993	Whitton United
1994	Grundisburgh
1995	Whitton United
1996	Needham Market
1997	Haughley United
1998	Grundisburgh
1999	Walton United
2000	Grundisburgh
2001	Grundisburgh
2002	Walsham-le-Willows
2003	Walsham-le-Willows
2004	East Bergholt United
2005	East Bergholt United
2006	East Bergholt United
2007	Grundisburgh
2008	Brantham Athletic
2009	Grundisburgh
2010	Old Newton United
2011	Grundisburgh
2012	Woodbridge Athletic
2013	Ipswich Valley Rangers
2014	Achilles
2015	Crane Sports
2016	Crane Sports
2017	Henley Athletic
2018	Achilles
2019	Crane Sports
2020	No title – Covid
2021	No title – Covid
2022	Henley Athletic
2023	Henley Athletic
2024	Henley Athletic

(* 1913 and 1914 – separate competitions run under Football Association and Amateur FA regulations)

Cambridgeshire League
(incomplete records)

1920	Newmarket Town
2011	Lakenheath

Essex/Suffolk Border League

1920	Haverhill Rov [West Division]
1948	Haverhill Rovers
1949	Sudbury Town
1950	Sudbury Town
1951	Stowmarket
1952	Sudbury Town
1953	Sudbury Town
1954	Sudbury Town
1955	Long Melford
1956	Long Melford
1957	Long Melford
1959	Long Melford
1961	Long Melford
1963	Haverhill Rovers
1964	Haverhill Rovers
1973	Brantham Athletic
1974	Brantham Athletic
1976	Brantham Athletic
1977	Brantham Athletic
1981	Sudbury Town (Reserves)
1989	Cornard United
1990	Sudbury Wanderers
1991	Sudbury Wanderers
2000	AFC Sudbury (Reserves)
2002	AFC Sudbury (Reserves)

Anglian Combination, Premier Division

1958	Lowestoft Town (Reserves)
1978	Lowestoft Town (Reserves)
1980	Lowestoft Town (Reserves)
2000	Kirkley
2002	Kirkley
2003	Kirkley

Step 7, Level 11
Anglian Combination, Division One

1975	Bungay Town
1976	Southwold United
1980	Kirkley
1981	Bungay Town
1985	Thetford Rovers
1988	Bungay Town
1989	Kirkley
1994	Lowestoft Town (Reserves)
2002	Beccles Town
2010	Kirkley/Pakefield (Reserves)
2016	Waveney

Other leagues
East Anglian League
(incomplete records)

1904	Ipswich Town
1935	Eastern Coachworks
1958	Lowestoft Town (Reserves)
1964	Lowestoft Town (Reserves)

Norfolk & Suffolk League

1898	Lowestoft Town
1899	Lowestoft Town
1901	Lowestoft Town
1902	Lowestoft Town
1903	Lowestoft Town
1904	Lowestoft Town
1929	Lowestoft Town
1931	Lowestoft Town
1938	Eastern Coachworks
1947	Bungay Town
1948	Bungay Town
1949	Bungay Town
1952	Bungay Town
1953	Beccles Town

North Suffolk League

1895	Kirkley
1896	Beccles Caxton
1897	Kirkley
1898	Lowestoft Town
1899	Lowestoft Town
1900	Lowestoft Town
1901	Lowestoft Town
1902	Kirkley
1903	Lowestoft Town
1904	Lowestoft Town
1905	Lowestoft Town
1906	Kirkley
1907	Beccles Caxton
1908	Kirkley
1909	Kirkley
1910	Gorleston [Norfolk]
1911	Lowestoft Town (Reserves)
1912	Morton's Athletic
1913	Leiston
1914	Leiston
1915-19	No competition
1920	Halesworth Town
1921	Halesworth Town
1922	Kirkley
1923	Lowestoft Town (Reserves)
1924	Kirkley
1925	Lowestoft Town (Reserves)
1926	Southwold Town
1927	Lowestoft Town (Reserves)
1928	Beccles Caxton
1929	Bungay Town
1930	Bungay Town
1931-33	No competition
1934	Eastern Counties United

Metropolitan League

1966	Bury Town
1969	Bury Town

That's champion!

Other leagues

Ipswich & Suffolk League

Formed: 1896 (as the Ipswich & District League)
Secretary: Mary Ablett *secretarysil1896@gmail.com*

Division One
Achilles – Salmet Close
Capel Plough – Red Lane
Cockfield United – Cockfield PF
Ipswich Wdrs Dev – SEH SG, Humber Doucy Ln
(AFC) Kesgrave – Ipswich School Sports Centre
Kesgrave Kestrels – Twelve Acre Approach
Kirton Athletic – Trimley S&SC
Saxmundham Sports – Sports Club, Carlton Road
Somersham – Main Road Playing Field
Stanton – Old Bury Road Recreation Ground
Thurston – Church Road Playing Field
Wenhaston United – Hall Road Playing Field
Woolverstone United – Hazelwoods, Marina Road

Division Two
Bacton United '89 Res – Brickwall Meadow
Claydon – Blue Circle Ground, Great Blakenham
Coplestonians Res – Copleston Centre, Foxhall Rd
East Bergholt United Res – Gandish Road PF
Elmswell – Blackbourne Community Centre
Framlingham Town A – Badingham Road
Gipping Gnats – Whitton Sports Centre
Halesworth Town Res – Dairy Hill
Redgrave Rangers – Church Way

Sporting '87 Res – Victory Sports Ground
Stonham Aspal – Rattlesden Playing Field
Trimley Red Devils Res – Stennetts PF
Wickham Market Res – Village Hall PF, off High St

Division Three
Cockfield United Res – Cockfield Playing Field
Coddenham Athletic – School Road
Coplestonians Dev – Copleston Cen, Foxhall Rd
Grundisburgh Res – Ipswich Road Playing Field
Haughley United Res – King George V PF
Henley Athletic Res – Church Meadows
Hope Church – Inspire Suffolk, Lindbergh Road
(AFC) Kesgrave Res – Ipswich School Sports Cen
Laxfield – Noyes Avenue Playing Field
Occold – Worlingworth Community Centre
Ransomes Sports Res – Sports Pav, Sidegate Ave
Samuels – Claydon & Barham Rec, Thornhill Road
Sporting '87 A – Victory Sports Ground

Division Four
Capel Plough Res – Red Lane, Capel St Mary
Debenham LC Res – Friends' Mdw, Gracechurch St
East Bergholt United A – Flatford Road
Hadleigh United Brettsiders – Layham Road SG
Ipswich Exiles – Bourne Vale Sports Club
(AFC) Kesgrave A – Ipswich School Sports Centre
Kesgrave Kestrels Res – Twelve Acre Approach
Leiston St Margaret's Res – Junction Meadow
Old Newton Res – Church Road PF
Redgrave Rangers Res – Church Way Sports Field
Stowupland Falcons Res – Church Road PF

Division Five
Achilles Res – Salmet Close
Bacton United '89 A – Brickwall Meadow
Benhall St Mary – School Lane
Bramford United – Acton Road Sports Ground
Brantham Athletic Dev – Tattingstone Playing Field
Brooks Hall Rovers – Whitton Sports Centre
Elmswell Res – Blackbourne Community Centre
Kesgrave Kestrels A – Kesgrave High School
Kirton Athletic Dev – Trimley S&SC
Mendlesham – Community Centre, Old Station Rd
Saxmundham Sports Res – Sports Club, Carlton Rd
Witnesham Wasps – St Audry's S&SC
Woolverstone Utd Res – Hazelwoods, Marina Rd

Anglian Combination (Suffolk teams)
Formed: 1964
Secretary: Chris McCullough
mccullough4321@gmail.com

Division Two
Beccles Caxton – Caxton Meadow
Beccles Town Res – College Meadow
Waveney Res – Saturn Close
Division Three South
Corton & Carlton Colville – Corton PF
Division Four South
Beccles Caxton Res – Caxton Meadow
Bungay Town Res – Maltings Meadow
Kirkley & Pakefield u23 – Walmer Road 3G
Lowestoft Town Res – Crown Meadow

Cambridgeshire County League (Suffolk teams)
Formed: 1908
Secretary: Phil Mitcham
phil.mitcham@cambridgeshirefa.com

Senior Division A
Haverhill Rovers Reserves – The New Croft
Hundon – Upper North Street
Senior Division B
Thurlow – Wratting Road, Great Thurlow
Division 1A
Exning United – Lacey's Lane Playing Field
Division 2A
Clare Town – Cavendish Road PF
Division 2B
(AFC) Mildenhall – Recreation Way
Division 3A
Haverhill Town – Mott's Field Playing Field
Haverhill Town A – Mott's Field Playing Field
Hundon Reserves – Upper North Street
Thurlow Reserves – Wratting Road, Gt Thurlow
Division 4A
Clare Town Reserves – Cavendish Road PF
Haverhill Town B – Mott's Field Playing Field
Haverhill Town Reserves – Mott's Field PF
Division 4B
Exning Utd Reserves – Lacey's Lane Playing Field
West Row Gunners – Beeches Road Playing Field

Other leagues

Essex & Suffolk Border League (Suffolk teams)
Formed: 1911 (merger of Colchester & District League and Colchester Borough League)
Secretary: Alison Stanford *esblsec@icloud.com*

Division One
Cavendish – The Sports Pavilion, Lower Street
Cornard United Res – Great Cornard SC
Great Bentley – Great Bentley Green

Division Two
Assington Stanley – Great Cornard SC
Boxford Rovers – Homefields
Great Bentley Reserves – Great Bentley Green

Lowestoft & District League (Suffolk teams)
Formed: 1900
Secretary: David Beecher
david.beecher@btinternet.com

Division One
Corton & Carlton Colville Dev – Corton PF
Kessingland – The Hive, Francis Road
Mutford & Wrentham Res – Wrentham PF
Normanston Magpies – Normanston Park
(AFC) Oulton – Dip Farm
Waveney Dev – Dip Farm

Division Two
Beccles Caxton Dev – Beef Meadow
Beccles Town A – Beef Meadow

Bungay Town u23 – Maltings Meadow
(AFC) Oulton Reserves – Dip Farm
Oulton United – Normanston Park
Waveney A – Dip Farm

Division Three
Flying Dutchman – Normanston Park
Kessingland Res – The Hive, Francis Road
Oulton United Res – Normanston Park
Pakefield Dynamos Dev – Ormiston Denes Acad
Southwold Town – Southwold Common

Central & South Norfolk League
Formed: 1905
Secretary: Derrick Johnson
derrick.johnson@hockeringfc.com

Division Two
Brandon Town Reserves – Church Road

Sunday Leagues
Bury & District Sunday League
38 teams in four divisions

Ipswich Sunday League
38 teams in four divisions

Norfolk Sunday League (includes Suffolk teams)
44 teams in five divisions

Other leagues
Lincolnshire Services League
17 teams in three divisions (including:)
RAF Honington – Heath Road, RAF Honington

Norfolk & Suffolk Veterans' League
58 teams in 10 divisions

Women's Leagues

FA Women's National League
Southern Premier Division
Ipswich Town – Dellwood Avenue, Felixstowe
Division One South East
AFC Sudbury – Brundon Lane
Reserve Division South East & Central
Ipswich Tn Dev – Ipswich Tn Acad, Playford Rd
AFC Sudbury Res – Brundon Lane

East Region Women's League
Premier Division
Needham Market – Bloomfields 3G
Division One North
Newmarket Town – Cricket Field Road

Suffolk Women's League
Premiership
Brantham Athletic – Brantham Leisure Centre
Bury Town Community – Ram Meadow
Capel Plough – Capel St Mary Playing Fields
(AFC Kesgrave) – Kesgrave High School
Needham Market Dev – Bloomfields 3G
Stowupland Falcons – Church Road
Woodbridge Town – Fynn Road

Championship
(Alresford Colne Rangers – Essex)
Bacton United '89 – Brickwall Meadow
Brantham Athletic Dev – Brantham Sports Centre
Coplestonians – Copleston High School
Framlingham Town – Badingham Road
Halesworth Town – Dairy Hill
Ipswich Valley Rangers – Westbourne Academy
Kesgrave Kestrels – Suffolk Constabulary Ground,
                            Main Road, Martlesham Heath
Leiston St Margaret's – Junction Meadow
(Ramsey & Mistley – Essex)
Saxmundham Sports – Sports Club, Carlton Road

Cambridgeshire Women's League
30 teams in three divisions (including:)
Haverhill Town – Mott's Field Playing Field
Newmarket Town Dev – Cricket Field Road

County FA contact details:

Suffolk County FA – Bill Steward House, The Buntings, Stowmarket, IP14 5GZ – 01449 616606
info@suffolkfa.com
www.suffolkfa.com

Cambridgeshire County FA – Bridge Road, Impington, Cambs, CB24 9PH – 01223 209 035
info@CambridgeshireFA.com
www.cambridgeshirefa.com

Essex County FA – Springfield Lyons Approach, Chelmsford, CM2 5LB – 01245 393078
greg.hart@essexfa.com
www.essexfa.com

Norfolk County FA – The FDC, Clover Hill Road, Norwich, NR5 9ED – 01603 704050 (Ext. 1)
info@NorfolkFA.com
www.norfolkfa.com

Selected defunct leagues

Beccles Caxtonian League – 1934-?
Brent Eleigh League – 1931-54
Bungay & District League – 1928-34
Bury & District League (St Edmundsbury League from 1995) – 1907-2019
Bury District Village League – 1921-60
Bury Minor League – 1948-50
Cockfield & District League – 1894-?
East Anglian League – 1908-64 (formerly South East Anglia League, merged with the Norfolk & Suffolk League to become the Anglian Combination)
Elm Valley League – 1987-?
Euston & District League – 1935-38
Eye & District League – 1946-56
Framlingham & District League – 1922-36
Hadleigh & District League – 1921-22
Halesworth District League – 1908-51
Harleston & District League – 1931-39 (A Norfolk league but with many Suffolk teams)
Haverhill & District League – 1899-1991
Ipswich District AFA League – 1910-14
Ipswich & District League – 1896-1978 (became Suffolk & Ipswich League)
Ipswich Junior League – 1907-46 (absorbed by the Ipswich & District League)
Ipswich War Time League – 1939-?
Leiston & District League – 1906-56

Lowestoft Rosary League – 1934-19
Lowestoft Wartime League – 1939-?
Mildenhall & District League – 1924-32
Nayland & District League – 1936-38
Norfolk & Suffolk League – 1897-1964 (merged with the East Anglian League to become the Anglian Combination)
North Suffolk League – 1894-1934
Norwich & South Norfolk League – 1977-2002 (A Norfolk league with several Suffolk teams. Merged with the Dereham & District League 1996 and the Central & South Norfolk League 2002)
Saxmundham & District League – ?-?
South Suffolk Junior League – 1906-53
Stowmarket District League – 1910-56
Sudbury & District Junior League – 1922-39
Sudbury & District League – 1898-1928
Walton & District League – 1929-31
West Suffolk League – 1894-1959
Wickhambrook & District League – 1922-48
Woodbridge District League – 1907-40

(Defunct league details courtesy of Non-League Matters Forum – nonleaguematters.co.uk)

The greatest day

FA Cup history was made on Saturday, May 6, when Suffolk-born Roger Osborne struck to give Ipswich Town a 1-0 victory over Arsenal at Wembley.

That is, so far, the only time a club from the county has lifted the famous trophy. The Tractorboys also reached the semi-finals in 1981 and the last-eight five times – in 1975, 79, 80, 85 and 93.

That was a long time since their first FA Cup appearance, way back in 1890 when a 2-0 win over Reading set them up for a run to the fourth qualifying round with further victories over Norwich Thorpe and Hunts County before going out 4-1 at home to 93rd Highland Regiment.

More than 40 teams from Suffolk have competed in the Cup since then, including several from local league level and others who have long since disbanded.

As for Wembley appearances, no Suffolk team has yet reached the FA Trophy final, although Sudbury Town were in the 1989 FA Vase final,

losing in a replay to Tamworth after a 1-1 draw beneath the famous Twin Towers.

AFC Sudbury were in the final three times on the bounce at the turn of this century but lost them all, 2-1 to Brigg Town at West Ham in 2003, 2-0 to Winchester City at Birmingham City the following year and 3-2 to Didcot Town at Tottenham Hotspur in 2005.

The losing streak was continued by Lowestoft Town, who went down 2-1 to Kirkham & Wesham at the new Wembley Stadium in 2008.

Further back in time, Lowestoft reached the 1900 FA Amateur Cup final but suffered a 5-1 defeat to Bishop Auckland at Filbert Street, Leicester.

Some of the Suffolk teams who have played in the FA Cup, together with their first and latest appearance (some are listed under more than one name).

Achilles 1949 – 50
AFC Sudbury 1999 – 2024
Beccles Caxton 1906
Beccles 1926, 58
Brantham Athletic 1939 – 2024
Bungay Town 1936 – 64
Bury St Edmunds 1901 – 23
Bury Town 1934 – 2024
Churchman Sports 1949 – 51
Cornard United 1994 – 2024
Debenham Leisure Cen 2007 – 16
Eastern Coachworks 1939 – 51
Eastern Counties United 1937
Exning United 1954 – 56
Felixstowe Town 1929 – 96
Felixstowe Port & Town 1997 – 2024
Framlingham Town 2017 – 21
Hadleigh United 1996 – 2024
Haverhill Borough 2014 – 19
Haverhill Rovers 1951 – 2023
Ipswich Old Grammarians 1947 – 49
Ipswich Town 1891 – 2024
Ipswich Works 1928 – 29
Kirkley 1900 – 35
Kirkley & Pakefield 2007 – 24
Kirkley & Waveney 1930 – 32
Lakenheath 2021 – 24

Leiston 1946 – 2024
Leiston Works Athletic 1920 – 35
Long Melford 1957 – 2024
Lowestoft Town 1899 – 2024
Mildenhall Town 2000 – 24
Needham Market 2003 – 24
Newmarket Town 1923 – 2024
Orwell Works 1923 – 39
RAF Martlesham 1933 – 39
Stowmarket 1932 – 86
Stowmarket Corinthians 1949 – 51
Stowmarket Town 1987 – 2024
Sudbury Town 1951 – 99
Sudbury Wanderers 1995 – 99
Team Bury 2010 – 15
Walsham-le-Willows 2006 – 24
Whitton United 1948 – 2023
Woodbridge Town 1996 – 2024

FA Trophy entrants:
AFC Sudbury 2006 – 25
Bury Town 1969 – 2025
Felixstowe & Walton Utd 2018 – 25
Haverhill Rovers 1969
Ipswich Wanderers 2023 – 25
Leiston 2011 – 25
Lowestoft Town 1969 – 25
Mildenhall Town 2017 – 25
Needham Market 2010 – 25
Newmarket Town 1969 – 2025
Stowmarket Town 1974 – 2024
Sudbury Town 1973 – 97

FA Vase entrants:
AFC Sudbury 1999 – 2006
Beccles 1978 – 82
Brantham Athletic 1979 – 25
Bungay Town 1974 – 84
Bury Town 1981 – 2006
Cornard United 1990 – 25
Crane Sports 1981 – 84
Debenham Leisure Centre 2006 – 23
Felixstowe & Walton Utd 2000 – 18
Felixstowe Town 1977 – 2000
Framlingham Town 2010 – 25
Hadleigh United 1979 – 25
Haverhill Borough 2013 – 25
Haverhill Rovers 1977 – 25
Ipswich Wanderers 1990 – 23
Kirkley & Pakefield 2007 – 25
Lakenheath 2019 – 25
Leiston 1987 – 2011
Long Melford 2003 – 25
Lowestoft Town 1984 – 2009
Mildenhall Town 1994 – 2024
Needham Market 1997 – 2010
Newmarket Town 1980 – 2024
RSSC Ransomes 1982 – 90
Stowmarket Town 1978 – 25
Sudbury Town 1984 – 99
Sudbury Wanderers 1992 – 99
Team Bury 2009 – 19
Walsham-le-Willows 2005 – 25
Whitton United 1996 – 24
Woodbridge Town 1991 – 25

FA Amateur Cup entrants:

Achilles 1947 – 71
Beccles 1949 – 62
Beccles Caxton 1898 – 1959
Beccles Town 1920 – 32
Brantham Athletic 1921 – 74
Bungay Town 1935 – 74
Bury St Edmunds 1898 – 1924
Bury Town 1924 – 58
Churchmans Sports 1949 – 53
Eastern Coachworks 1937 – 55
Eastern Counties United 1936
Electric Supply & Transport 1955
Felixstowe Town 1929 – 73
Felixstowe United 1947 – 53
Hadleigh United 1954 – 61

Halesworth 1899 – 1907
Haverhill Rovers 1907
Ipswich Electricity Supply 1947 – 68
Ipswich Old Grammarians 1946 – 49
Ipswich St John 1927
Ipswich Town 1893 – 1936
Ipswich Wanderers 1950 – 61
Ipswich Works 1920 – 28
Kirkley 1896 – 1935
Kirkley & Waveney 1929 – 32
Lakenheath 1937 – 53
Landseer 1954 – 64
Leiston 1900 – 73
Leiston Works Athletic 1919 – 35
Long Melford 1931 – 53

Lowestoft Town 1898 – 1957
Orwell Works 1907 – 64
RAF Felixstowe 1931 – 39
RAF Martlesham Heath 1932 – 39
St Clement's United 1947
Stoke United 1947 – 50
Stowmarket 1912 – 73
Stowmarket Corinthians 1948
Stowupland Corinthians 1946 – 48
Sudbury 1897
Sudbury Town 1912 –50
Waterside Works 1950 – 66
Whitton United 1947 – 73
Woodbridge Athletic 1952 – 57
Woodbridge Town 1927 – 33

From left: The FA Vase and FA Trophy on the pitch at Wembley Stadium, FA Cup and FA Amateur Cup.

There are some competitions that are always guaranteed to have a Suffolk winners – the various county cups (although how Cambridge Town snuck in to win in 1910 is a mystery!).

The Suffolk County Football Association was formed in 1885, with 11 founder members: Beccles College, Bury School, Bury Town, Cowell's Club (Ipswich), Framlingham College, Ipswich Association [now Ipswich Town], Ipswich Rangers, Ipswich School, Stowmarket, Sudbury Town and Woodbridge Town.

Suffolk Senior Cup

1886	Woodbridge	1910	Cambridge Town	1938	Bury Town	1967	Felixstowe Town
1887	Ipswich Town	1911	Suffolk Dist Asylum	1939	Bury Town	1968	ICI
1888	Long Melford	1912	Ipswich Town	1940-45	No competition	1969	Hadleigh United
1889	Ipswich Town	1913	Ipswich Town		Second World War	1970	Waterside Works
1890	Ipswich Town	1914	Ipswich Town	1946	Bury Town	1971	Crane Sports
1891	Framlingham College	1915-19	No competition –	1947	Lowestoft Town	1972	Hadleigh United
1892	Beccles College		First World War	1948	Lowestoft Town	1973	Heath Row
1893	Beccles Caxton	1920	Beccles Town	1949	Lowestoft Town	1974	Crane Sports
1894	Framlingham College	1921	Long Melford	1950	Bungay Town	1975	Felixstowe Town
1895	Long Melford	1922	Beccles Town	1951	Stowmarket Town	1976	Brantham Athletic
1896	Ipswich Town	1923	Lowestoft Town	1952	Stowmarket Town	1977	Nicholians
1897	Beccles Caxton	1924	Lowestoft Town	1953	Long Melford	1978	Woodbridge Town
1898	Beccles Caxton	1925	Kirkley	1954	Long Melford	1979	Ransomes
1899	Beccles Caxton	1926	Lowestoft Town	1955	Long Melford	1980	Nicholians
1900	Ipswich Town	1927	Brantham Athletic	1956	Lowestoft Town	1981	Ransomes
1901	Kirkley	1928	Ipswich Town	1957	Sudbury Town	1982	Crane Sports
1902	Kirkley	1929	Ipswich Town	1958	Stowmarket Town	1983	Hadleigh United
1903	Lowestoft Town	1930	Ipswich Town	1959	Whitton United	1984	Crane Sports
1904	Ipswich Town	1931	Stowmarket Town	1960	Brantham Athletic	1985	Bury Town (Reserves)
1905	Ipswich Town	1932	Lowestoft Town	1961	Bungay Town	1986	Westerfield United
1906	Ipswich Town	1933	Stowmarket Town	1962	Stowmarket Town	1987	Sudbury Tn (Reserves)
1907	Ipswich Town	1934	Stowmarket Town	1963	Whitton United	1988	Grundisburgh
1908	Ipswich Town	1935	Newmarket Town	1964	Grundisburgh	1989	Cornard United
1909	Long Melford	1936	Stowmarket Town	1965	Stowmarket Town	1990	Needham Market
		1937	Bury Town	1966	Oulton Broad	1991	Sudbury Wanderers

1992	Whitton United
1993	Woodbridge Town
1994	Woodbridge Town
1995	Grundisburgh
1996	Grundisburgh
1997	Haverhill Rovers
1998	Grundisburgh
1999	Walton United
2000	Grundisburgh
2001	Kirkley
2002	Kirkley
2003	Long Melford
2004	Hadleigh United
2005	Needham Market
2006	Walsham-le-Willows
2007	Stowmarket Town
2008	Grundisburgh
2009	Beccles Town
2010	Team Bury
2011	Whitton United
2012	Whitton United
2013	Ipswich Wanderers
2014	Whitton United
2015	Lakenheath
2016	Waveney
2017	Achilles
2018	Woodbridge Town
2019	Achilles
2020	Ipswich Wanderers
2021	Lakenheath
2022	Ipswich Wanderers
2023	Framlingham Town
2024	Trimley Red Devils

Suffolk Junior Cup

1890	Ipswich Town (Res)
1891	Halesworth
1892	Bungay Chaucer Press
1893	Landguard Fort
1894	Kirkley
1895	Leiston
1896	Beccles Red Star
1897	Woodbridge OSM
1898	Kirkley (Reserves)
1899	Brantham Athletic and Lowestoft Tn (Reserves) – joint winners
1900	Mildenhall
1901	Lowestoft Town (Res)
1902	Haverhill Rovers (Res)
1903	Lowestoft IOGT
1904	Southwold
1905	Orwell Works
1906	Halesworth Town
1907	Ipswich Town (Res)
1908	Stowmarket
1909	Woodbridge
1910	Orford
1911	Sudbury Brigade Utd
1912	All Saints United
1913	not known
1914	Stoke Athletic
1915-20	No competition
1921	St Mary Elms Old Boys
1922	Egerton Amateurs
1923	Lowestoft Town (Res)
1924	Halesworth Town

1925	Leiston St Margaret's
1926	Woodbridge Town
1927	Newmarket Town (Res)
1928	Brantham Ath (Res)
1929	Utd Svcs (Lowestoft)
1930	Old Nactonians
1931	Exning United
1932	Melton St Andrew's
1933	Kirkley (Reserves)
1934	Eastern Co's Utd (Res)
1935	Eastern Co's Utd (Res)
1936	Eastern Co's Utd (Res)
1937	Lakenheath
1938	RAF Mildenhall
1939	Beccles Town
1940-45	No competition
1946	Brooke Marine
1947	Lowestoft Town (Res)
1948	Lowestoft Town (Res)
1949	Leiston St Margaret's
1950	Lowestoft Town (Res)
1951	Bury East Athletic
1952	Brandon Town Street
1953	Landseer Youth Club
1954	Lowestoft CWS
1955	Brandon Town
1956	Grundisburgh
1957	Beccles Caxton
1958	Beccles Caxton
1959	Beaconsfield
1960	Castle Hill Youth Club
1961	Southwold Town
1962	Honington School

1963	Oulton Broad
1964	Finningham
1965	Finningham
1966	Finningham
1967	Brandon Town
1968	Finningham
1969	Finningham
1970	Old Lowestoftians
1971	Woodbridge Town
1972	Lake Lothing
1973	St Edmund's RCYC
1974	Murrayside
1975	Lakenheath
1976	Alan Road
1977	St Edmund's RCYC
1978	St Edmund's RCYC
1979	Murrayside
1980	St Edmund's RCYC
1981	Brandon Town
1982	Post Office Research
1983	Leiston
1984	Leiston
1985	Needham Market
1986	Ashlea
1987	Woodbridge Town
1988	Walsham-le-Willows
1989	Walsham-le-Willows
1990	Walsham-le-Willows
1991	Saxmundham Sports
1992	Newbury United
1993	Newbury United
1994	Stanton
1995	Wenhaston United

1996	Haughley United (Res)		
1997	Cavendish		
1998	Tuddenham Rovers		
1999	Tuddenham Rovers		
2000	Tuddenham Rovers		
2001	Bramford United		
2002	Westerfield United		
2003	Cockfield United		
2004	Hearts of Oak		
2005	Leiston St Margaret's		
2006	AFC Sudbury (Res)		
2007	Stonham Aspal		
2008	Old Newton United		
2009	Achilles		
2010	Bacton United '89		
2011	Glemsford & Cavendish United		
2012	Westerfield United		
2013	Oulton Broad		
2014	Coplestonians		
2015	Ipswich Athletic		
2016	AFC Hoxne		
2017	Bacton United '89		
2018	AFC Kesgrave		
2019	Bildeston Rangers		
2020	Halesworth Town		
2021	Stowupland Falcons		
2022	Stowupland Falcons		
2023	AFC Kesgrave		
2024	Woolverstone United		

Suffolk Premier Cup

Year	Winner	Year	Winner
1959	Bury Town	1980	Lowestoft Town
1960	Bury Town	1981	Sudbury Town
1961	Bury Town	1982	Sudbury Town
1962	Bury Town	1983	Sudbury Town
1963	Stowmarket Town	1984	Brantham Athletic
1964	Bury Town	1985	Sudbury Town
1965	Bury Town	1986	Stowmarket Town
1966	Bury Town	1987	Sudbury Town
1967	Lowestoft Town	1988	Sudbury Town
1968	Ipswich Town	1989	Sudbury Town
1969	Ipswich Town	1990	Sudbury Town
1970	Ipswich Town	1991	Stowmarket Town
1971	Bury Town	1992	Sudbury Town
1972	Lowestoft Town	1993	Sudbury Town
1973	Sudbury Town	1994	Newmarket Town
1974	Sudbury Town	1995	Newmarket Town
1975	Lowestoft Town	1996	Bury Town
1976	Sudbury Town	1997	Newmarket Town
1977	Sudbury Town	1998	Sudbury Wanderers
1978	Bury Town	1999	Newmarket Town
1979	Lowestoft Town	2000	Lowestoft Town
		2001	Lowestoft Town
		2002	AFC Sudbury

2003	AFC Sudbury
2004	AFC Sudbury
2005	Lowestoft Town
2006	Lowestoft Town
2007	Ipswich Tn (Reserves)
2008	Needham Market
2009	Lowestoft Town
2010	Ipswich Tn (Reserves)
2011	Bury Town
2012	Lowestoft Town
2013	Bury Town
2014	Bury Town
2015	Lowestoft Town
2016	Lowestoft Town
2017	Needham Market
2018	Leiston
2019	Leiston
2020	Needham Market
2021	No final – Covid
2022	Needham Market
2023	Needham Market
2024	Needham Market

Premier Cup
Proudly sponsored by
Endeavour Automotive

Senior Cup
Proudly sponsored by
CNet Training

For the latest county cup news, visit the www.suffolkfa.com/cups-and-competitions web page.

Did you know?

● One of the most unusual goals ever recorded in Suffolk football came in 1890 during Lowestoft Town's 3-1 win at Gorleston and caused the match 'umpire' to walk off in disgust. In the days of no nets and crowds right up the touchlines, incursions on to the pitch were common. It resulted in the scorers being listed as Neubronner 1, J Bly 1 and 'small boy 1' after a young lad ran on and forced a loose ball into the goal.

● When Bury Town moved from Kings Road to Ram Meadow in 1978, they took with them their supporters hut, which is still serving snacks today.

● In the early days of football at Long Melford, the ball was an animal bladder covered in Hessian. The village launched a Penny a Week campaign to buy the club's first leather ball.

● In the early days of Hadleigh United, the players' tin baths were filled up from the neighbouring River Brett.

● A meeting in Ipswich Town Hall in 1878 resulted in the formation of Ipswich AFC. They began playing at Broom Hill before ousting the town's rugby club from its pitch in Portman Road. At Broom Hill, players used a shed at the Inkerman pub across the road as a dressing room

● Brantham Athletic went 72 years between FA Cup appearances. After losing 4-0 at Crittall Athletic in 1938, they did not play again until beating Woodbridge Town 4-2 in 2010.

● One of Long Melford's earliest players was capped for England at football and played county cricket for Kent. William Nevill 'Nuts' Cobbold played in most of the club's earliest matches and was selected for national duty as centre forward between 1883 and 1888. He scored twice on his debut in a 7-0 win against Ireland, going on to score six times in nine games. The Cambridge Blue was nicknamed Prince of Dribblers. He played once for Kent and also represented his university at tennis.

● Stowmarket made extensive use of the railway to travel to away games. However, on one occasion, thanks to the River Gipping then being navigable, went by barge for a match in Ipswich.

● Walsham-le-Willows' Summer Road pavilion, which is still in place, used to have a thatched roof. Water was carried to it using a two-wheeled hand water cart pulled by the players.

● Bury St Edmunds FC defender Reginald De Courtney Welch played for the club in 1877. He had been a member of The Wanderers side that won the first FA Cup in 1872 and also played for England against Scotland in the world's first official international match later that year.

● Former FIFA president Sir Stanley Rous was born in Mutford and played as goalkeeper for both Kirkley and Lowestoft. He went on to referee the 1934 FA Cup final and 34 international matches. He also served as Football Association secretary from 1934 until 1962.

Did you know?

- Bury Town's former Kings Road ground was the first in East Anglia to operate floodlights when the Blues played a floodlit game against Cambridge City in January 1953 in front of 2,105 spectators.

- Football legend Stan Mortensen turned out for Newmarket Town in the East Anglian League during the Second World War.

- During the 1920s, Mildenhall Town players got changed in the local town hall before home games and then proceeded to the ground with a band playing in front of them.

- Until 1959 the Cock & Bell public house was used as Long Melford's headquarters and changing rooms. The players had to walk along the village main street for games at Stoneylands.

- Stowmarket Town parked 11 lorry trailers alongside their Cricket Meadow pitch in 1951 to act as extra viewing areas for their FA Amateur Cup tie against Romford. It helped accommodate a record 3,338 crowd.

- Access to Haverhill Rovers' former Seven Acres ground was via a railway bridge. Neither the ground nor railway now exists. Rovers moved from there to Hamlet Croft in 1926 and now play at The New Croft.

- When Stowmarket Town moved from their old Cricket Meadow ground to Green's Meadow in 1984, they took with them some of the turf and wooden terracing, which had originally been bought from Ipswich Town in the early 1950s.

- Beccles Town's ground record did not involve their own team. It was set for the 1955/56 Suffolk FA Premier Cup semi-final between Bungay Town and Lowestoft Town, when 3,000 packed into College Meadow.

- Lowestoft Town used to play at Denes Oval – literally a long throw-in from the sea. The club's first dressing rooms were a clubhouse bought from the Royal Norfolk & Suffolk Yacht Club at the turn of the 1900s. It was transported a mile to Crown Meadow and served until 1989.

- The first match programme known to be issued by Ipswich Town was in the 1923/24 season for the visit of Essex-based Old Parkonians in the Southern Amateur League.

- When Bury Town moved from Kings Road in 1976, the new Ram Meadow ground was not ready. It meant they had to play the 1976/7 season on an unenclosed site at Hardwick Heath.

- Newmarket Town bought their ground from the town's cricket club for £800 in 1959. The two sports shared the ground until 1985 when the cricketers moved out, ending its three-sided situation.

- Both of Bungay Town's grounds have been in Norfolk. They moved from the Recreation Ground to their current Ditchingham base in 1953. They have, however, played some home games in Suffolk – using Outney Common and Honeypot Meadow when the Rec was flooded. Honeypot Meadow is now under the town's police station.

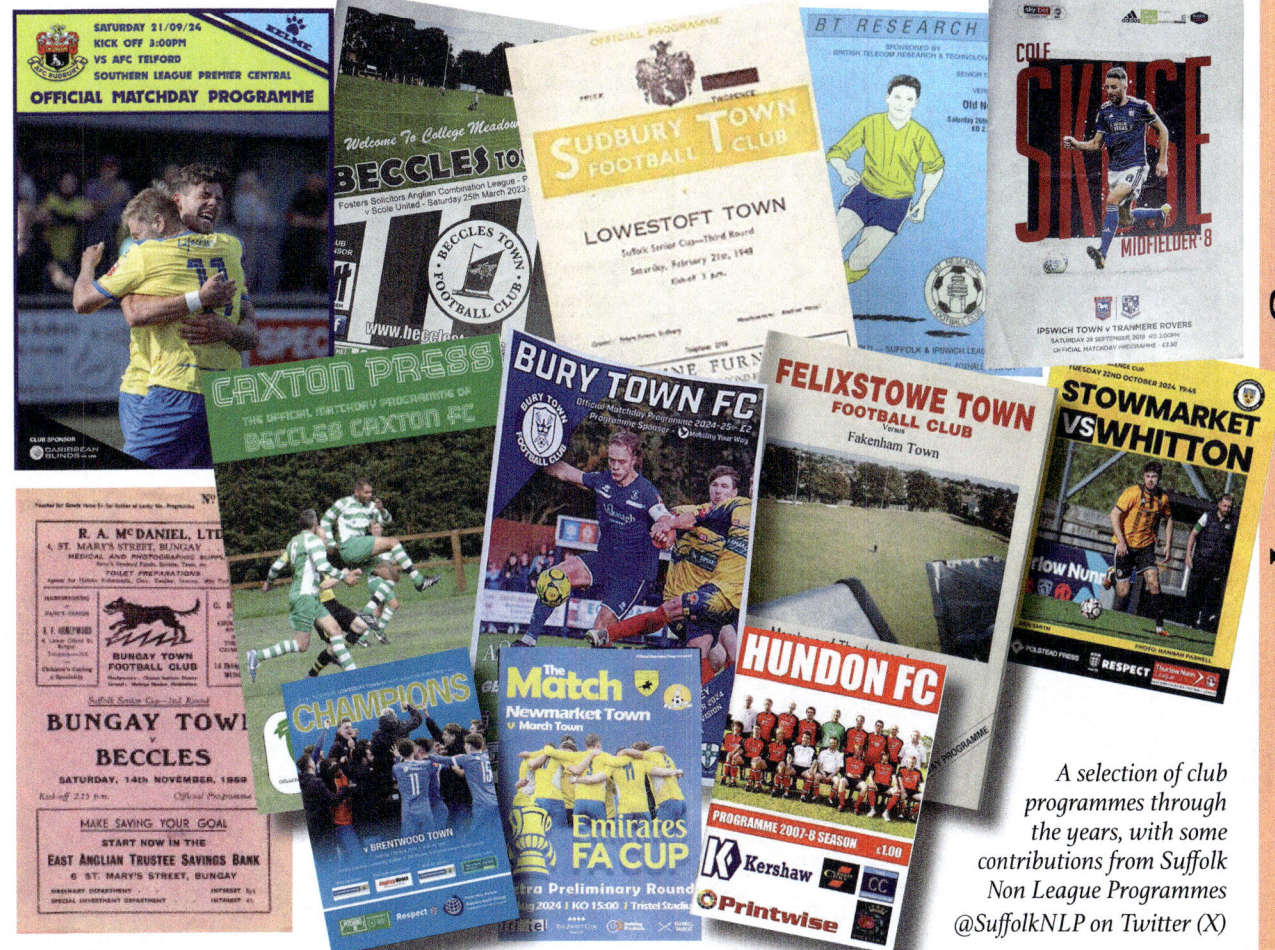

A selection of club programmes through the years, with some contributions from Suffolk Non League Programmes @SuffolkNLP on Twitter (X)

Programme parade

The Offside Trust

In November 2016, British football was rocked by a series of high-profile revelations regarding child sexual abuse. Several former professional players bravely waived their right to anonymity to speak out about their past abuse.

A number of those involved, decided to set up the Offside Trust, an organisation committed to supporting survivors and working to make sport safer for children.

Former professional footballer Steve Walters is director of the Offside Trust and ambassadors include former youth player Gary Cliffe (Manchester City) and Alan Arber (Norwich City) as well as professional boxer Callum Hancock.

Former Coventry and Millwall player Billy Seymour was also an ambassador but sadly passed away in 2019. Several others are involved but wish to remain anonymous.

The Offside Trust is run by survivors, for survivors and is an independent body working alongside clubs, organisations and other charitable bodies to further enhance safeguarding at all levels of sport.

Its aims are:
● To raise awareness of the importance of safeguarding across all sports at all levels
● To provide survivors with advice, guidance and resources to aid the healing journey
● To campaign for legal and regulatory changes to improve safeguarding in sport

The Offside Trust is run by a dedicated band of volunteers.

The trust is not a charity, which means it can freely lobby politicians and campaign for legal changes around safeguarding. It is a not-for-profit organisation and reinvest all funds raised into the delivery of its aims and objectives.

The trust is building partnerships with clubs and charities, so that it can make the greatest difference where it is needed most.

The trust's objectives are:
● To secure partnerships with clubs at all levels, in all sports
● To engage with survivors and signpost them to the appropriate professional support
● To engage with survivors within the Offside Trust Support Network
● To support charitable helplines with a specific focus on survivors in sport

The Offside Trust

- To change the law on child sexual abuse being exempt from 'Double Jeopardy'
- To lobby for 'Mandatory Reporting' to be adopted in UK law
- To engage with political and judicial bodies to strengthen legal support for survivors

Since 2016, the Offside Trust has received the support of supporters, clubs, players and former professionals throughout the sporting world.

The trust focuses on all sports, not just football, and is grateful for the support given by people in cricket, rugby, golf and boxing, among others, to help raise further awareness.

Find out more about The Offside Trust on its website – *www.offsidetrust.com*

Leaflets are widely distributed to reach anyone affected.

The FA has commissioned a dedicated NSPCC helpline for adults who were abused in childhood within the football industry, from grassroots to Premier League. To speak to somebody, the free helpline for guidance and support is available 24 hours a day on **0800 023 2642.**

Survivors Manchester (*www.survivorsmanchester.org.uk*) and Samaritans (*www.samaritans.org*) have help and support available for anyone needing to talk.

If you think a child is in immediate danger, always dial 999.

If you are a child who needs help, call Childline on 0800 11 11.

To contact The Offside Trust directly send a direct message on X (Twitter) @OffsideTrust or email *alan.offsidetrust@gmail.com* for further information.

Awareness of The Offside Trust is spreading throughout Suffolk

Thank you

The author is grateful to the fantastic volume of help offered by individuals, clubs and organisations across Suffolk for their assistance in the compilation of this book.

Thanks go to them all, as well as the many people on social media who replied to my requests and were happy to fill in missing details and accommodate my visits to their grounds.

Huge thanks go to Brian Bunn for access to his so-far-unpublished East Anglian league tables book to fill gaps in the North Suffolk League history.

Thanks too to my son Jordan for his artistic skills in being able to pull together my low-quality pictures and sketches of team shirts and transform them into something wonderful.

A special expression of gratitude goes to Alan Arber at The Offside Trust, who kindly agreed to be the book's associate partner. The work the organisation does is incredible and I am happy to give them a wider platform.

Apologies if I've missed anyone out but rest assured your input was equally valued.

In the modern age, research is so much easier thanks to the internet and the following websites are highly recommended: the Football Club History Database (*fchd.info*), Football Grounds in Focus (*footballgroundsinfocus.com*), Wikipedia (a handy first point of reference, just double check the facts!) and the many club, league and FA websites serving football in the county so well.

Any errors are mine. Please let me know of any you spot and they will be corrected in any reprints.

Bibliography

A History of Haverhill Rovers by Roy Brazier
An English Football Internationalists' Who's Who by Douglas Lamming
FA Cup 150 by Phil Annets
Five Score – The SIL Football Book of the Century by KP Wood
Echoes Across Crown Meadow – the history of Lowestoft Town FC 1888-1997 by Mike Pearce
Homes of Non-League Football by Peter Miles
Non League by Bob Barton
Non-League Football Tables of the East of England 1896-2023 by Michael Robinson
The FA Cup Complete Results by Tony Brown
The FA Amateur Cup Complete Results by Fred Hawthorn
The History of Non-League Football Grounds by Kerry Miller
The Ultimate FA Trophy and FA Vase Statistics Book by Tony Brown

Advance subscribers

Grateful thanks go to the following people who kindly paid in advance for On the drag. Your support is much appreciated.

- James Ager, Ipswich, Suffolk
- David Austin, Bourne, Lincolnshire – *always pleased to visit Suffolk*
- *Happy memories* – Gifford Baxter, Lowestoft, Suffolk
- Glyn Beck, Northallerton, North Yorkshire
- David Boon, Creeting St Mary, Suffolk
- John Bramley, Barton-upon-Humber, Lincolnshire
- John Bryant, Ipswich, Suffolk
- In memory of George Calver (Coddenham Athletic)
- 'Catch' – Ipswich, Suffolk
- Craig Cooper, Leiston, Suffolk
- *"Always thinking of Reg"* – Steve Coulson, Bishop's Stortford, Hertfordshire
- Neil Daniel, Scarborough, North Yorkshire
- Mick Docking, Huddersfield, West Yorkshire

- Alan Douglas, Newport, Wales
- Gary Dourado, Haverhill, Suffolk
- Andy English, Lavenham, Suffolk
- Mike Fields, Diss, Norfolk
- Ian Howitt, Benfleet, Essex
- *Here's to another successful county-based grounds book, following on from Pilgrims' Patch (Lincolnshire)* – Martyn Girdham, Winterton Rgrs FC
- Neil Harvey, Cambridge
- Mark Horseman, Cheltenham, Gloucestershire
- Russell Kanharn, Lakenheath, Suffolk
- Ben Kilhams, Hemel Hempstead, Hertfordshire
- *For my dad Robert Holt an avid Grimsby Town supporter and my biggest role model!* – Sophie Lamping, Mildenhall, Suffolk
- *For Mickey Lamping, from a small town in Illinois. I convinced him to go to his first proper football game (Lakenheath) in the UK. I may have finally ended the soccer/football debates in the house!*
- Tony Lees, Chippenham, Wiltshire

- Bob Lilliman, London
- Colin Little, Felixstowe, Suffolk
- Phil Maskell, Lowestoft, Suffolk
- *Uppa Caxton* – Shaun Mayston, Beccles, Suffolk
- Paddy Mooney, Birmingham
- Glenn Parfitt, Ipswich, Suffolk
- Alasdair Ross – Ipswich supporter and hopper
- Richard Simons, Aylsham, Norfolk
- Paul Tricker & Family, Mickfield, Suffolk
- Nigel Silk, Chatteris, Cambridgeshire
- Ian Sparrow, Addlestone, Surrey
- Mark Timbury, Taunton, Somerset
- Joel Windsor, Flowton, Suffolk
- A non-League football fan – Sale, Cheshire

- Bury Free Press (Suffolk Sport)
- East Anglian Daily Times & Star
- Suffolk County FA
- Suffolk & Ipswich League

Also by this author

Pilgrims' Patch – The football grounds of Lincolnshire

Discover the football grounds and fields of Lincolnshire, including a 'flashback' section reliving the teams and grounds of the past . **£19.95 from Amazon** *(£18 direct from publisher)*

Island Hopping – The football grounds of Lanzarote

Heading for the sunshine this winter? Find out everything you need to know about football on Lanzarote. **£15.99 from Amazon** *(£13 direct from publisher)*

Tarts, Trams and Tuk Tuks – A Lisbon football weekend

Discover the delights of football and more in and around the Portuguese capital. After an opening night's death-defying dash only to be refused entry by a belligerent security guard it had to get better… didn't it? Available direct from the author via eBay – **£7.50 from Amazon** *(£6 direct from publisher)*

Soap Stars & Burst Bubbles
Amazon £11.24 (£9.99 e-book)

Towering Tales & a Ripping Yarn
Amazon £12.24 (£9.99 e-book)

The Mont
Amazon £16 (£12 direct from publisher)

The Totty Cup
Amazon £26 (£20 direct from publisher)

Order direct – https://tinyurl.com/spennymedia

Printed in Great Britain
by Amazon

59661397R00106